Wealth and Poverty in Early Christianity

Wealth and Poverty in Early Christianity

Helen Rhee

Fortress Press
Minneapolis

WEALTH AND POVERTY IN EARLY CHRISTIANITY

Cover image: The Offering of the Poor Widow (Luke 21:1-4). Early Christian mosaic, 6th CE./Alfredo Dagli Orti / Art Resource, NY

Cover design: Laurie Ingram

Print ISBN: 978-1-4514-9641-3

eBook ISBN: 978-1-5064-2559-7

The paper used in this publication meets the minimum requirements of American National Standard for Information Sciences — Permanence of Paper for Printed Library Materials, ANSI Z329.48-1984.

Manufactured in the U.S.A.

This book was produced using Pressbooks.com, and PDF rendering was done by PrinceXML.

Contents

Series Foreword

In his book *The Spirit of Early Christian Thought*, Robert Louis Wilken reminds us that "Christianity is more than a set of devotional practices and a moral code: it is also a way of thinking about God, about human beings, about the world and history" (xiii). From its earliest times, Wilken notes, Christianity has been inescapably ritualistic, uncompromisingly moral, and unapologetically intellectual.

Christianity is deeply rooted in history and continues to be nourished by the past. The ground of its being and the basis of its existence are the life of a historic person, Jesus of Nazareth, whom Christians identify as God's unique, historical act of self-communication. Jesus presented himself within the context of the history of the people of Israel, and the earliest disciples understood him to be the culmination of that history, ushering in a new chapter in God's ongoing engagement with the world.

The crucial period of the first few centuries of Christianity is known as the patristic era or the time of the church fathers. Beginning after the books of the New Testament were written and continuing until the dawn of the Middle Ages (ca. 100–700 CE), this period encompasses a large and diverse company of thinkers and personalities. Some came from Greece and Asia Minor, others from Palestine and Egypt, and still others from Spain, Italy, North Africa, Syria, and present-day Iraq. Some wrote in Greek, others in Latin, and others in Syriac, Coptic, Armenian, and other languages.

This is the period during which options of belief and practice were accepted or rejected. Christian teachers and thinkers forged the language to express Christian belief clearly and precisely; they oversaw the life of the Christian people in worship and communal structure, and clarified and applied the worshiping community's moral norms.

Every generation of Christians that has reconsidered the adequacy of its practice and witness and has reflected seriously on what Christians confess and teach has come to recognize the church fathers as a precious inheritance and source for instruction and illumination. After the New Testament, no body of Christian literature has laid greater claim on Christians as a whole.

The purpose of this series is to invite readers "to return to the sources," to discover firsthand the riches of the common Christian tradition and to gain a deeper understanding of the faith and practices of early Christianity. When we recognize how Christian faith and practices developed through time we also appreciate how Christianity still reflects the events, thought, and social conditions of this earlier history.

Ad Fontes: Sources of Early Christian Thought makes foundational texts accessible through modern, readable English translations and brief introductions that lay out the context of these documents. Each volume brings together the best recent scholarship on the topic and gives voice to varying points of view to illustrate the diversity of early Christian thought. Entire writings or sections of writings are provided to allow the reader to see the context and flow of the argument.

Together, these texts not only chronicle how Christian faith and practice came to adopt its basic shape, but they also summon contemporary readers to consider how the events, insights, and social conditions of the early church continue to inform Christianity in the twenty-first century.

George Kalantzis
Series Editor

Introduction

The issue of wealth and poverty for Christian faith is as ancient as the original Jesus movement and reaches farther back to ancient Israelite thought and practices reflected in the Hebrew Scriptures. As frequently noted, Jesus's teachings in the Synoptic Gospels demanded a kind of discipleship that barred any competing commitment to people or things other than himself, including money and possessions. From the very beginnings of the Christian movement, how to deal with riches formed an important aspect of Christian discipleship and was thought to express "an essential articulation of our faith in God and of our love for our fellow humans."[1] Early Christians believed that the Christian attitude toward and use of wealth was a critical identity marker that distinguished Christians from non-Christians in their Greco-Roman context. However they theologized riches and poverty, they had to grapple with and respond to the clear call of the social and material responsibilities of the gospel.

This volume is designed to introduce the reader to the broad range of texts that reflect early Christian thoughts and practices on the topic of wealth and poverty. The selected texts from the second to the fifth centuries show not only their chronological development but also their regional spread and diversity in relation to the growing institutionalization and

---

1. L. T. Johnson, *Sharing Possessions: Mandate and Symbol of Faith* (Philadelphia: Fortress, 1981), 16.

other doctrinal developments in the church. They also show how early Christians adopted, appropriated, and transformed the Jewish and Greco-Roman moral teachings and practices of giving and patronage, as well as how they developed distinctive theologies and social understandings of wealth/the wealthy and poverty/the poor. The texts' variety of genres such as a revelation, novel, apology, polemic, theological treatise, sermon, letter, biography, and a biblical commentary represents a contextual character of their teachings, thoughts, or practices expressed on the one hand, and an overarching unity and consistency of themes discussed on the other. In general, the main concern of these texts and early Christian leaders was wealth and the wealthy rather than poverty and the poor. In light of the Gospels' apparent "preferential option for the poor," wealth, not poverty, presented the serious theological and moral problem in the sociology of the early church.[2]

A word about translation is in order. I have used existing modern English translations for several texts in the volume with permissions. I have also updated and revised existing English translations based on the primary sources for some with permissions. I translated the rest. Both for the revised and translated texts, I tried to strike a balance between contemporary language and literal translation. I also used gender-inclusive language when appropriate while trying to be sensitive to the authors' historical and cultural (patriarchal) contexts. The biblical quotations were translated from the documents themselves (i.e., the Septuagint[3] and the Old Latin versions) and display some significant differences from modern English translations, including modern chapter-and-verse divisions for the Old Testament.

---

2. C. Lindberg, *Beyond Charity: Reformation Initiatives for the Poor* (Minneapolis: Fortress, 1993), 22.

3. The Septuagint is translation of the Hebrew Bible into Koine Greek, a process that took from the third century BCE to the first century BCE; it is typically indicated by the Roman numeral LXX, "seventy." The Old Latin versions used in the Western church were translated from this. The Septuagint included other Hellenistic Jewish literature of the Second Temple period not part of Hebrew Bible, which is known as the (OT) Apocrypha. Early Christians regarded and engaged with it, including those additional texts, as Scripture.

This introduction intends to provide the reader a general overview of the socio-economic and theological and moral contexts of early Christians in which the selected documents were written. It also introduces the authors and the texts more concretely to the reader.

The Greco-Roman Context and the New Testament[4]

Early Christians were part of a larger Greco-Roman world and lived and operated within the existing social, economic, political, religious, and cultural framework of the Mediterranean world dominated by the Roman Empire. Roman economy was an advanced agrarian economy: predominantly a subsistence economy largely based on agriculture (75–80 percent) with relatively solid technological development and market exchanges. Agriculture, business, and trade were based on scarcity and mainly used for consumption and self-sufficiency. As in other ancient and traditional societies, a dominant economic and cultural ethos was that of limited good: that any desirable good (such as wealth, health, land, honor, friendship, respect, status, power, privilege, etc.) existed in finite quantities; thus a person or family could acquire or increase these goods only at the expense of others. In this worldview, the only practical ways to acquire wealth naturally (i.e., justly or innocently) was through inheritance or production for self-sufficiency through agriculture or crafts; trade (except in a large scale) was usually associated with pettiness and greed for its goal of making profit (as opposed to self-sufficiency). Therefore, the rich or those getting richer were usually seen in a negative light by the moralists. This general ethos is reflected in the embedded nature of Roman economy and its values and systems of social distinctions and hierarchy. The enormous structural inequalities constituted the very fabric of sociopolitical stratification and the values that governed the economic behaviors of various social groups.

---

4. In this section I draw on H. Rhee, *Loving the Poor, Saving the Rich: Wealth, Poverty, and Early Christian Formation* (Grand Rapids: Baker Academic, 2012), ch. 1.

The Roman socio-economic hierarchy consisted of imperial and aristocratic elites (1–3 percent), a middle group[5] with moderate surplus resources (7–15 percent), and the "poor," who were either stable near subsistence (22–27 percent), at subsistence (30–40 percent), or below subsistence (25–28 percent). As one can see, while the term "poor" is a relative term, 82–92 percent of the population still lived near or at subsistence level, struggling for survival and sustenance, particularly vulnerable to natural disasters and diseases.

A way to reinforce the hierarchy *and* deal with social and economic inequalities was a patronage system. Based on the ethics of reciprocity, it worked between (usually) men of unequal power or status. The patron, the social superior, provided his client, the dependent, with protection and economic and political benefits (such as food, land, housing, recommendations, appointments to office, and even inheritance); the client in return was obliged to return the favor with loyalty, votes, and praise, which enhanced the patron's honor and status. Access to the center of power was mediated through such relationships as patronage presupposed and thrived on competition for scarce power resources on the one hand and desire for enhancement of status and honor on the other. The emperor was the patron par excellence for the whole empire, providing the plebs (freeborn citizens) with basic urban amenities such as food, water, housing, baths, and entertainment. However, aristocrats also practiced their patronage in smaller but no less significant ways. In addition to personal patronage, they provided public benefactions for their respective cities, towns, and countryside throughout the empire (e.g., baths, libraries, water, theaters, games, and festivals) for love of honor and love of their cities/hometowns—so that they would garner gratitude and honor in return and thus maintain and enhance their power and status.

The recipients of these public benefactions—which evidently were not designed to relieve poverty—were identified

---

5. I use this phrase rather than a "middle class" since there was no distinct "middle class" in a modern sense in the (ancient) Roman world.

as the members of particular civic communities, including the privileged elite, and the recipients' needs were not considered favorable factors in distribution. Justice meant that each should receive proportionally to one's status, not one's need; therefore, the (working) poor, though ubiquitous, received gifts as "justice" demanded only if they were part of and participated in the civic community, and the destitute and beggars were excluded from the civic community. Thus the poor were ever-present but largely remained invisible.

While the Greco-Roman rich and moralists disregarded the poor and poverty in general, they were concerned with wealth and the ethics of wealth. Philosophers and moralists regarded generosity as the quintessential virtue of a good aristocratic man and love of wealth (greed/avarice), which manifested either in miserliness or prodigality (luxury), a classic vice. Following Aristotle, they regarded money as sterile and valuable only for its utility as a medium of exchange. Therefore, usury (i.e., lending with interest to make money through money) and its accumulation (including other wealth) were unnatural and manifestations of greed.

Although early Christians engaged with these socio-economic realities and moral teachings, they primarily inherited the Israelite and Jewish teachings and practices from the Hebrew Scriptures (the Septuagint).[6] The Torah (Pentateuch) reveals Yahweh's absolute ownership of the earth and affirms the goodness of the physical creation and material prosperity as God's blessings to the righteous for their obedience. The Torah also underscores God's special care and protection for the poor, widows, orphans, and strangers in a covenant community by establishing social obligations toward them. While the Wisdom tradition also affirms wealth as God's blessings, it relativizes its value in relation to wisdom with its attendant danger; it further enjoins the rich to do justice, be generous to the poor, and care for them, and warns them of dishonesty involving wealth. Reflecting the changing situations of emergence of plutocratic landowners and the deepening impover-

6. See n. 3.

ishment of the majority of the population under the monarchy, the Prophets fiercely denounced the wealthy and powerful for their idolatry and its byproduct: their social and economic injustice and oppression of the poor in particular.

The prophetic oracles against the oppressive rich can be juxtaposed with the psalmists' self-identification with the poor and needy, most frequently in psalms of lament, who are the victims of the wicked and suffer from the latter's injustice and oppression. Being helpless and needy, the poor cry out and turn to God for help and appeal to God's righteousness and salvation; God is the just defender and protector of the poor and deliverer of the oppressed. The notion of poverty, then, is extended to the religious and spiritual level, and the poor are identified as the humble, the afflicted, the oppressed, and the righteous who turn to God for help and enjoy God's special favor. This emerging notion of "the pious poor and the wicked rich" developed significantly in the post-exilic Second Temple period, especially with the emerging genre of apocalypse, such as the apocryphal literature included in the Septuagint. This literature envisioned a "great reversal" of the respective earthly fortunes of the pious poor and the wicked rich in the last day. At the same time, the apocryphal wisdom literature in the Septuagint, such as Sirach and Tobit, furthered the theme of the righteous rich who were generous to the poor and protected them along with widows and orphans. Sirach and Tobit also prioritized almsgiving in three forms of Jewish piety (with prayer and fasting), suggesting its salvific or atoning efficacy. All of these social, political, and theological developments would profoundly affect early Christian understandings of and practices involving wealth and poverty and the rich and poor.

In first-century Palestine, the concentration of wealth in the hands of a small group of pro-Roman landed aristocracy and the general impoverishment of the majority of the population (the landless peasants) fueled a serious volatility in the context of Roman occupation. Believing that the eschatological new age had indeed dawned with Jesus, his early followers inherited the tradition of "the pious poor and the oppressive rich."

In the Gospels, while Jesus associates with the wealthy and powerful and is often a recipient of people's hospitality and financial support for his itinerant ministry, he speaks to his disciples (and the crowds) about the antithesis between serving wealth (*mamōnas*) and serving God (Matt 6:24; Luke 16:13); he tells the rich young man (ruler) to sell his possessions, give the proceeds to the poor, and follow him to inherit eternal life (Matt 19:21; Mark 10:21; Luke 18:22). Whereas the poor are the recipients of Jesus's good news and beatitude with a promise of God's kingdom (Matt. 5:3; 11:5; Luke 6:20; 7:22–23), Jesus pronounces woe to the rich (Luke 6:24) and a virtual impossibility for the rich to enter God's kingdom (e.g., Matt. 19:24). As he warns of the lure of wealth (e.g., Mark 4:19), he stresses laying up lasting heavenly treasure rather than perishable earthly treasure by giving alms (Luke 12:33; cf. Matt 6:19–20).

As noted by most scholars, the Gospel of Luke (and the book of James) places its emphatic concern and favor on the poor, and a strong disapproval on the rich and their wealth in a series of stories unique to Luke. Turning traditional Greco-Roman reciprocity and patronage upside down, Jesus commands the host of the feast to invite not the relatives or rich neighbors but the poor and disabled, pointing to the latter's place at the great eschatological banquet (14:13, 21). The parable of the rich fool (12:16–21) shows the folly of the rich man's avarice and security in possessions, which is a sign of his spiritual poverty, while the story of the rich man and Lazarus (16:19–31) dramatizes the great eschatological reversal between them. Whereas both the rich fool and the rich man fail to care for the poor and consider God while on earth, Zacchaeus, a "sinful rich publican," receives Jesus's pronouncement of salvation apparently through almsgiving to the poor and making restitution for ill-gotten wealth (19:1–10). Jesus himself exhorts his disciples to "make friends for [themselves] with dishonest wealth" for their eternal abode (16:9 NRSV).

Although the early Christian groups did not formally identify themselves as the "poor," in general they belonged to the lower strata and the "poor" in varying degrees living near, at, or below subsistence both in Palestine (e.g., Jesus and disciples; the Jerusalem church) and outside Palestine (Pauline communities) with a few exceptions. In particular, the early Jerusalem assemblies in Acts had special concerns for meeting the needs of the community members: they held all things in common and redistributed possessions to all according to one's need, to the effect that "there were no needy persons among them" (2:42–47; 4:32–37). This, by the way, hardly suggests that these assemblies practiced "communism" in an anachronistic, modern political-economic sense. While members of Paul's urban communities were predominantly plebs (free laborers and artisans), slaves, and recent immigrants, one would find a degree of (at least) moderate wealth in the house churches: that is, the middle group of the relatively prosperous—those who could offer their places for assemblies and hospitalities for Paul and his associates and act, therefore, as "patrons" for the communities (e.g., Phoebe in Rom 16:1–2; Gaius in Rom 16:23; 1 Cor 1:14; Philemon in Phlm 1–2).

In this context, the standard Pauline teachings are charity (good works) and hospitality for fellow believers, which are shared by the rest of the New Testament (Heb 13:2, 16; 1 Pet 4:9; 3 John 5–8). These teachings follow traditional Jewish piety based on the concern and activity of God and Christ: caring for the poor (Gal 2:10); working with one's own hands as to avoid idleness and dependence (Eph 4:28; 1 Thess 4:11–12; 2 Thess 3:6–12); warnings against greed (1 Cor 5:11; 1 Tim 3:8; Titus 1:7); and generosity and hospitality toward others, particularly fellow believers (Rom 12:8, 13; 1 Cor 16:2; 2 Cor 8:2; Eph 4:28), rooted in Christ's own generosity (2 Cor 8:9). Especially important for Paul was his collection for the needy believers in Jerusalem (Rom 15:26, 31; 1 Cor 16:3; 2 Cor 8:14; cf. Gal 2:10) as a demonstration of unity between Jewish and gentile congregations and therefore the legitimacy of his apostolic ministry (to the gentiles), among other reasons. In the (later) Pastoral letters, Christians are exhorted to "do good works/deeds" (i.e., almsgiving/charity for those in need) (Titus 2:14, 3:8; cf. Gal 6:9–10, "to work the good"); and the rich believers are especially commanded to be humble, put their hope in God rather than in the uncertainty of riches, and practice generosity (1 Tim 6:17–18), which will result in spiritual blessing in the age to come (1 Tim 6:19).[7] Warnings against "love of money" and "pursuing dishonest gain" are prominent for qualifications for church leadership (1 Tim 3:3, 8; cf. 6:10; Heb 13:5a; 1 Pet 5:2) in direct contrast to descriptions of false teachers and the people in the last days as "lovers of money" and those seeking "dishonest gain" (2 Tim 3:2, 4; Titus 1:11; cf. 2 Pet 2:3, 14). In the Pauline letters, there are further adaptations from Greco-Roman moral teachings of the time: the importance of "cheerful giving" (2 Cor 9:7), contentment (1 Tim 6:6–8; cf. Heb 13:5a), and self-sufficiency (*autarkēs*) in all circumstances (Phil 4:11; cf. 1 Tim 6:7–8).

The Second and Third Centuries

No longer an insignificant religious movement from Palestine, the Christian church in this period witnessed significant external and internal growth. With distinctively "gentile Christianity," it experienced substantial but uneven growth especially in the urban centers of the Greek-speaking world (especially Asia, Egypt, and Greece), Syria, and the Latin West (Italy and North Africa in particular).

In terms of its social advancement, some major missionary activities were directed to the members of the upper strata, especially in Alexandria, Syria, Rome, and North Africa, and converts to Christianity came from several social spectra. Despite pagan critic Celsus's scorn that Christianity attracted only the uneducated, slaves, outcasts and women,[8] the Christian social make-up resembled in fact the typical social pyramid of the Roman Empire: a vast majority in the lower strata, with a growing minority from aristocratic elite and sub-elite middling groups (especially in the third century). The emergence of the refined Christian apologists in the late second

---

7. For spiritual blessings in this life, see 2 Cor 9:10–15; Phil 4:14–20.
8. Origen, *Against Celsus* 3.44, 55.

century points not only to the development of Christian literary culture but (at least a beginning of) Christian penetration into the educated rank of the society, which disturbed and threatened the conservative pagan elites; philosophers such as Celsus and Porphyry took up Christianity as a worthy target for both their philosophical and social polemic. Furthermore, particularly prominent were the conversions of high-status women, the remarkable orientation of Christians to literary texts and activities, and their increasing financial and organizational capacity, which could indicate some fair number of Christians from the top 10 percent of Roman society. While we should be careful not to exaggerate Christian penetration into the conservative upper echelon during this period, it is important to recognize Christianity's appeal to a socially mobile group of people and the rank and file of the Roman society, and also the upward social mobility of Christians and consequently increasing social gaps and tensions among individuals within Christian communities.

Christians during this period produced growing bodies of literature, later grouped as the Apostolic Fathers, apologies, treatises, and more radical apocryphal Acts. These attest to how early Christians interpreted and applied for their community contexts and concerns the sayings of the Lord and the letters of the apostles—which eventually came together as the New Testament—while they were still "strangers" in the Empire. As evidenced in these bodies of literature (including the New Testament), salvation for early Christians was a corporate phenomenon in that it occurred within a community context and necessarily entailed social responsibility (as well as cultivated personal virtues) as a testament to faith in God and Jesus Christ. Indeed, the early church proclaimed that Jesus Christ was the Savior whose revelation of God and sacrifice on the cross provided his followers the once-for-all atonement for sin that began a life of faith through baptism. In the second century, baptism, which marked a new beginning, was increasingly thought of as a "seal of salvation" that brought about remission of sins, rebirth, and the gift of the Holy Spirit. This salvation, a life-long process, would involve and demand a steady progress in "taking off an old self and putting on a new self" and the persistent cultivation of spiritual and ethical virtues in community. And this moral and spiritual advance and transformation (without which salvation is incomplete) entailed both internal and external works of faith that would attest to one's faith in God. Thus, for enacting this theology, bridging the internal social gaps and tensions, and meeting the intra-community and inter-community needs, there were universal calls for sharing material resources (*koinōnia*) and almsgiving with an increasing salvific significance, especially in dealing with the problem of sin after being baptized. By the mid-third century, as a growing institution, the church centralized its charitable ministries under the supervision of the clergy—the bishops in particular. The two documents and the three authors in this volume represent these emerging, multi-faceted thoughts and practices on wealth and poverty in this period.

The Shepherd of Hermas

The Shepherd of Hermas, which is grouped in the collection known as the "Apostolic Fathers," was one of the most popular books of early Christianity and was included in some regional canons of the New Testament in the second through the fourth centuries. The Shepherd of Hermas narrates a series of revelations or visions and exhortations given by angelic figures (first, the elderly woman representing the church, and then the shepherd, the angel of repentance) to Hermas, a Christian living in Rome in the first half of the second century. Arranged into five visions, twelve commandments, and ten parables, the book deals with (perceived or real) internal issues of the local Christian community in apocalyptic form and style. It is especially concerned with the thorny problems of sin after baptism and repentance, and the behavior of the rich and their relationship to the poor within the community. Can Christians have a chance to repent and be forgiven if they sin after their baptism? The Shepherd's answer is yes, but only once and for a limited time, so one must repent quickly before it becomes too late. This represented a moderate position in the early church, striking a balance between God's justice and mercy, between rigorism and leniency.

A second, related issue that contributed to the community's internal crisis is the spiritual complacency of certain wealthy believers[9] resulting from their preoccupation with wealth and business activities and the social disparity between the rich and poor. In a series of visions of the cosmic tower (i.e., the eschatological church), the danger of wealth is its attachment to the present world, which keeps people preoccupied with their own security and well-being to the neglect of their social responsibility of caring for the needy. In our selected texts, eschatological salvation and wealth are not compatible unless the latter is "cut away" from the rich. However, those who repent "quickly" by seeking out the hungry and doing good with their wealth, "until the tower is finished," will enter the kingdom (albeit with difficulty). The parable of the two cities, reflecting conceptual contrasts between this world and the next, between heavenly and earthly riches, conveys a message that Christians should not pursue this-worldly wealth but other-worldly through the care of the afflicted. Thematically, this leads to our last selection, the famous parable of the elm and the vine, which envisions mutual cooperation and dependence between the rich and the poor in preparation for the world to come. Based on the traditional notion that the rich are deficient in the things of God due to their wealth and distraction while the poor are rich in intercession and praise with effectual power, only working together, as do the fruitful vine and the barren elm, may rich and poor support and benefit each other through their respective services for the coming judgment. The goal of these visions and parables is not to denounce wealth or the rich as such but to move the rich into concrete behaviors for the good of the community (and thus for their own good).

---

9. Probably those in a middle group.

Clement of Alexandria

Clement of Alexandria, one of the first Christian apologists and theologians in the second century, was born around 150 CE in Athens. After conversion to Christianity, Clement became a student of Pantaenus, who was the first head of a catechetical school at Alexandria in Egypt and whom he succeeded around 200. This school became one of the most renowned theological centers, and when Clement fled to Cappadocia, in 202 or 203, during the persecution under emperor Septimius Severus, he was succeeded by Origen. Of the four extant works of Clement, three form a trilogy on Christian life: the *Exhortation to the Greeks* (*Protreptikos*), a classic apology for Christianity urging educated non-Christians ("Greeks") to convert to Christianity as a new philosophy; *Christ the Instructor* (*Paedagogos*), best understood to be a handbook for new converts and catechumens in which Christ, the Divine Instructor, guides them in the moral precepts of Christian faith; and lastly, the *Miscellanies* (*Stromata*) expounds the faith to mature Christians by defending the use of classical wisdom to interpret true Christian knowledge (*gnōsis*). In all these works, Clement sees the compatibility between Christianity and the best of Greek civilization and philosophy (i.e., Platonism and Stoicism) and shows his own familiarity with them and dexterity in using them for the life of a true Christian "gnostic" (i.e., a perfect Christian) in the journey of salvation.

For our purpose, Clement's most relevant work is his pastoral homily, *The Rich Man's Salvation* (*Quis dives salvatur*, literally *Who Is a Rich Man That Is Saved?*), from the end of the second century. Addressed to the affluent and cultured Christian audience in Alexandria, the salvation of the rich—who could identify with the "rich young man" in Mark 10:17–31—emerges as a considerable theological and social challenge that needs to be reinterpreted and reapplied. To the rich man's quest for eternal life, Jesus responded with an apparent demand to dispossess of his wealth and, ultimately, declared the virtual impossibility for the rich to enter the kingdom of God *as the rich*. Is there hope for the rich, then? If so, how can they be saved? Clement acknowledges that salvation seems to be more difficult for the rich than the poor, but he wants to show the *concerned* rich who *have already been initiated* into the salvation process "how what is impossible with humans becomes possible" (2)—with Christ's instruction of the truth and their good works in lifelong perseverance. Clement spiritualizes wealth and poverty as well as the rich and the poor through a figurative interpretation of the Scriptures and deconstructs the traditional notion of the pious poor and the wicked rich; both the rich and poor share the capacity for and responsibility of moral choice of detachment and spiritual freedom but are also subject to the temptation of greed and attachment to wealth. However, he also relies on the spiritual superiority of the poor and difficulty of salvation for the rich to stress the symbiotic relationship between their respective roles, just like the Shepherd's parable of the elm and the vine—the rich giving alms generously to the poor who would, in turn, intercede to God for their spiritual destiny. For the rich, almsgiving is a necessary part of the care of the self, which is indispensable for the journey of salvation, the path to perfection.

Therefore, as in other matters such as marriage and sexuality, Clement chooses a *via media* ("middle way") of sustained almsgiving based on the utility of wealth against both a non-Christian adulation of obsession with wealth, and heterodoxical (gnostic and encratite) renunciation and dispossession of wealth as a norm for all Christians.

The Acts of Thomas

The Acts of Thomas comes from the early third century in East Syria, where a distinctive form of Christianity developed and most likely produced the Gospel of Thomas and the Book of Thomas as well. Judas Thomas, the "Twin Brother of Jesus," is the principal mediator and carrier of a Christian tradition in these three works that also share the dualistic and encratic[10]

---

10. See the first sentence of the next paragraph for its principal meaning.

theology of their Syrian milieu. Originally written in Syriac, the Acts of Thomas survives in its entirety only in Greek[11] and narrates the missionary travels, miracles, preaching, persecution, and martyrdom of Judas Thomas in a similar fashion to Greco-Roman novels. As early as the late third century, this Acts and the other apocryphal acts of the time[12] were gathered as a corpus by the Manichaeans[13] in place of the canonical (Lukan) Acts of the Apostles.

Known for its encratic message and in contrast to the "middle way" of Clement of Alexandria, the Acts portrays the "superiority" of Christian sexual morality and ethos, with the exaltation of virginity and radical sexual continence on the one hand and the condemnation of marriage and sexual intercourse on the other. We find a similar (but not identical) parallel in its treatment of wealth and poverty: riches are the other "linchpins" of the present age that bound people to earth. While the dangers of wealth and possessions are placed in contrast to heavenly riches and earthly riches, a call for their renunciation to the convert is not as consistent as that of sexual renunciation. On the other hand, a connection between almsgiving and conversion/salvation is well established, especially with the intriguing story of Thomas building a palace for King Gundaphorus, which suggests a substitutionary effect and efficacy of almsgiving even for a non-Christian benefactor. Wealth and poverty within this dualism also affects its understanding of Christ. The Acts shows a particular interest in portraying Jesus as a poor one (on earth) yet a generous dispenser of true (heavenly) riches. This portrayal of Christ seems to be a natural outworking of the apostle Paul's description of Christ in 2 Corinthians 8:9. While the incarnation itself is an act of condescension and poverty, Jesus's earthly life of poverty, out of

11. While scholars note various degrees of gnostic characters or tendencies in each of these works, those gnostic tendencies do not warrant them to be classified as gnostic texts per se.
12. Particularly the Acts of Andrew, the Acts of John, the Acts of Paul, and the Acts of Peter.
13. The Manichaeans were the dualistic and encratic religious group (with some Christian elements) founded by the Persian Mani in the late third century. Augustine of Hippo participated in this religion for ten years prior to his conversion to Neo-Platonism and then to Christianity.

which his spiritual riches are offered, is assumed and taken for granted. This theme will eventually develop as a popular motif in the writings of the post-Constantinian church fathers as well as the spiritual Franciscans in the medieval period. Thomas's credibility as the bearer of this particular tradition of Christianity, then, rests in main part upon his poverty, as a true imitator of Jesus, and therefore as a true mediator between God (Christ) and the present world.

Tertullian

In the North African scene, we find Tertullian, an elite Christian apologist and theologian[14] at the turn of the third century (c. 193–220 CE), and Cyprian, the refined and charismatic bishop of Carthage in the mid-third century (d. 258 CE). Both were adult converts of high birth, with classical education, significant resources,[15] and demonstrative familiarity with the sophisticated literary culture of Carthage. Tertullian's many writings are typically divided into four groups: the apologetical works, passionately defending Christianity often against Roman African culture; the polemical writings, fiercely attacking heretics; the moral writings, explaining Christian virtues and disciplines; and the sacramental ones, writing about Christian rites such as baptism. While he established fundamental theological language for trinity, Christology, church, and sacraments for Western theology, Tertullian was also known for his theological and moral rigorism, identifying himself with the New Prophecy ("Montanism") and becoming even stricter later in his understanding of Christian theology and practices in his own Carthaginian context.[16]

Tertullian's view of wealth, scattered in his works, conforms to his overall vision of Christianity as the specific manifestation of and testament to Christian identity, conduct, and real-

14. Tertullian was also the first Christian theologian to write in Latin as well as Greek.
15. It was certainly more so for Cyprian than Tertullian.
16. Recent scholarship rightly highlights the continuity and development of Tertullian's theology in his context as suggested here rather than Tertullian's stricter stance in New Prophecy per se or in a stricter form of New Prophecy.

ity in the Roman world. Christian appearance, discipline, good works, and merit as external means of ascertaining Christian truth and faith are crucial indicators of the internal state of the soul and absolutely critical and integral to one's salvation. For this reason, Tertullian gives meticulous attention to disciplinary matters, even matters of spectacles, modesty, veiling, dress, ornaments, and the soldier's crown in his treatises. In this context, wealth, which is essentially granted by God but is fraught with dangers, temptations, and problems to souls and human relationships, presents Christians with a unique challenge and opportunity to demonstrate their spiritual state and persevere in their salvation and thereby distinguish themselves from pagans.

Tertullian takes up the issue of wealth, the rich, and the poor in the first selection, his anti-heretical polemic *Against Marcion*. There he defends the fundamental unity of God in the Old and New Testaments as both the Creator and the Redeemer against Marcion's dichotomy between the two and radical asceticism in rejection of the material world. In this context, Tertullian points out that God the Creator, who out of his generosity supplied the Israelites with material provisions and made Solomon rich, does grant material things and riches to his people. God and money are antithetical and while God does condemn boastfulness of riches; however, Christ, who showed the unity of God, rather than ridding money away from God's service advises us to use worldly possessions to procure ourselves future friendships and support, that is, eschatological salvation (on Luke 16:1–17). Concerning Jesus's discourse with the rich man in (Luke 18:18–22), almsgiving was the one commandment of God put forth by Jesus to the rich man to compensate for a lack in the Old Testament law, and as such it made one's redemption attainable. Furthermore, for Tertullian, both Testaments (as the Scripture is one) are straightforward and consistent in "God's preferential option for the poor." He takes for granted the pious poor and oppressive rich tradition and does not allegorize or spiritualize wealth and poverty or the rich and the poor, as Clement of Alexandria does.

In the second text, *On Patience*, Tertullian deals with greed (*cupiditas*)—the desire of money (1 Tim 6:10)—in the context of addressing Christian patience in the face of many ills in life, including the loss of property. On the one hand, Jesus, who himself was poor and always justified the poor and condemned the rich (7), is a model of patience through his indifference toward money. On the other hand, this greed is an acquisitive spirit, which by nature is never satisfied with one's own wealth but always crosses a boundary of one's "private property" for something that belongs to another and to God. Hence, when a Christian is unable to bear his or her material loss, he or she sins directly against God (7) since greed is essentially an offence to God's sovereign ownership and a false and pretentious claim to non-ownership. Therefore, just as patience is a virtue that defines the Christian's relationship with God and his/her "neighbors," impatience in loss is a vice that disrupts and eventually destroys both vertical and horizontal relationships.

Cyprian of Carthage

Moving to the mid-third century, there is none who champions the triangular relationship of riches and poverty, almsgiving, and salvation better than Cyprian, who admired Tertullian. Upon his conversion to Christianity around 246 CE, Cyprian dispensed almost all his wealth for the relief of the poor and was elected bishop (albeit with some opposition) just two years later. The political catastrophes, socio-economic problems, natural disasters, and ecclesiastical crises and schisms of his time included the two imperial persecutions of Decius (250–251) and Valerian (257–258) and the terrible plague of 252–254, and provided the important context for his eschatological sensitivity and social and moral teachings. During the Decian persecution of 250 and 251, Cyprian conducted his ministry through letters from a hideout while a mass apostasy (or *lapse*) of the wealthy Christians in particular troubled the church of Carthage. Upon his return to the city at the end of the persecution, Cyprian faced the ensuing problems of the confessors[17] granting reconciliation to some of those wealthy *lapsi* and the open rebellion of dissenting clergy.

In *On the Lapsed* (251), Cyprian sees the persecution (however evil that may be) rather as God's testing of his household, which had been growing complacent in the years of peace. Cyprian attributes a cause for the persecution and mass apostasy to the rich Christians' greed (*cupiditatis*) and attachment to their possessions to the neglect of generous charity for the needy (5–8, 11). Cyprian speaks of them as slaves to profit and money, tethered to the chain of their wealth (12). To them he provides the "apostolic solution": scorn worldly possessions and leave them for the kingdom of God and heavenly compensation (12). Cyprian frames both the problem and the solution in apocalyptic dualism with a sense of urgency, for the end of the world was at hand with the Judgment of Christ. As the sign of true repentance, the (wealthy) lapsed should apply themselves frequently "to almsgiving, by which souls are freed from death" (35; cf. Tob 12:8). Cyprian urges them to invest their earthly goods and riches with the Lord, their coming judge (35), a practice that could allow them to be readmitted and reconciled to the church.

In *On Works and Almsgiving*, which was probably written during the deadly and devastating plague that came suddenly after the persecution, Cyprian develops the strongest theological argument yet for "redemptive almsgiving," with greater rigidity in his attitude toward wealth and the wealthy and more pronounced concern for the care of the poor.

The plague of 252–254 was another demoralizing blow to Christians who had just gone through the imperial persecution, especially those Christians who felt that the sweeping deaths by the plague had stripped (or would strip) them of the

17. Both confessors and martyrs were Christians who remained faithful and "confessed" their faith in Christ during the persecutions. Although the distinction was often blurred in practice, the term "confessors" came to refer to those who survived the persecution and its attendant punishment (imprisonment, torture, condemnation to mines, etc.) while "martyrs" were those who perished by capital punishment (decapitation, death by gladiators or beasts) or torture.

possibility of either a second chance for salvation (reconciliation) or perfection through martyrdom.[18] Cyprian addressed their anxiety and pessimism and pointed them to another way to purge sin other than martyrdom: almsgiving to the poor—not as heroic as martyrdom but certainly effective (6). For Cyprian, far from being a human work in danger of threatening or supplanting the exclusive divine work of salvation, almsgiving was God's own mercy and design, which provided for God's people this particular wayout for their post-baptismal sins. Jesus's death and almsgiving never compete with each other, and the latter does not undermine the salvific significance or sufficiency of the former. Both are expressions of God's abundant grace, condescension, and providence, and it is only by God's grace that almsgiving can be meritorious and satisfactory in God's sight (1, 2, 5). Like Clement of Alexandria and the author of the Acts of Thomas, Cyprian audaciously describes it as an economic transaction (which is to be repeated often in the subsequent centuries). Givers of alms are "merchant[s] of the heavenly grace" whose gain is none other than eternal life (7) in partnership with Christ (13) and who make God their debtor (15, 16, 26). For Cyprian, almsgiving as lifelong penance provided an absolutely necessary (pre-)condition *for and with* the reconciliation of the lapsed, and their "conspicuous almsgiving" would be a means that should sustain the care of the poor in his congregation, which was financially strapped due to persecution and schism. Thus, earthly "riches offered the remedy for the very harm they caused" for the wealthy.[19] *On Works and Almsgiving* was widely circulated and became foundational in the Western church in the centuries to follow.

---

18. *Mortality* 17. Although the early church generally opposed voluntary martyrdom, it made an exception for the lapsed Christians who needed to "wash away their former fault" (apostasy) through offering themselves up for martyrdom, and Cyprian himself attested to its occurrence (Letter 24); see also *Laps.* 36.
19. W. Countryman, *The Rich Christians in the Church of the Early Empire: Contradictions and Accommodations* (Lewiston, NY: Mellen, 1980), 189.

Lactantius

Lactantius lived in the second half of the third century through the first quarter of the fourth century (c. 250–325 CE) and joins Tertullian and Cyprian as an illustrious North African Christian rhetorician and apologist. A brilliant orator, he was first named an official chair in Latin rhetoric at Nicomedia by the emperor Diocletian (284–304) but was soon dismissed at the start of the Diocletian persecution ("the Great Persecution") in 303; he then served as tutor for Constantine's son Crispus during the Great Persecution (303–313). Later called "the Christian Cicero" due to his elegant style, Lactantius became an effective advocate for his newfound religion, drawing on and engaging with the classical authors. Lactantius wrote the *Divine Institutes* during the Great Persecution to set forth the true doctrine and worship, that is, Christianity, against the falsehood of pagan religion and tradition. As such, it was a forerunner of Augustine's much more substantial and sophisticated counterstrike to paganism in the *City of God* (c. 412–426).

In the *Divine Institutes*, Lactantius develops a coherent body of Christian ethical thinking in dialogue with and against classical thought. In the selected texts, he brings together justice and true worship. For Lactantius, chief marks of justice are true worship (*pietas*) and equity or fairness (*aequitas*): if people do not worship the true God, they do not know or practice justice. Then, only Christians, who believe in the true God, can understand and practice acts of justice and its derivative, equity or fairness (*aequitas*), as the natural consequences of their true religion. Civil justice (i.e., Greco-Roman pagan justice), derived from relative and utilitarian civil laws, is not really justice at all, due to Greco-Roman polytheism (paganism) and its consequent social inequality. In contrast, natural justice, which derives from God's single, uniform rule, is true justice because of divine reward and retribution at the judgment (*Inst.* 5.18). Only natural justice breeds true equity, which is not necessarily social but essentially spiritual, and resides therefore only in true religion, Christianity (5.15). Everyone has equal standing before God in the sense that God judges inner dispositions and virtues, not outer status markers or distinctions. Thus Lactantius understands private property and economic distinctions compatible with Christian justice and *aequitas*.

The key to achieving and acting out Christian justice and *aequitas* in the present (in his society) is service to fellow humans. Lactantius believes that the common bond of humanity (*humanitas*) should generate a sense of solidarity and compassion (*misericordia*) for one another and is a basis of equality (6.10). In this, Lactantius debunks a deeply seated Greco-Roman custom of reciprocity and patronage by linking Greco-Roman reciprocity to *utilitas*, the basis of the unjust civil law. In contrast, Christian generosity and charity should be directed to "the unsuitable" as far as possible, "because a deed done with justice, piety and humanity is a deed you do without expectation of return" (6.11). Thus, equality in the present is something that is true irrespective of social and economic distinctions but demands that the works of justice be directed to the poor and the desperate ("the needy and the useless") entirely irrespective of their worthiness and reciprocity. Well before the passionate arguments of the Cappadocian Fathers and John Chrysostom in the East, and Ambrose and Augustine in the West, Lactantius championed the humanity of "the needy and the useless."

The Fourth and Fifth Centuries[20]

When Constantine seized the imperial power in the West with the power of the Christian God (312 CE), the church had been functioning as a formidable social and economic institution with a massive operation of charity, as already suggested. Constantine's unprecedented imperial patronage of the church did not prompt a brand new theological base for the work the church had been doing, which by then had been securely established, but it transformed the scale, way, and impact that the church's charity and wealth had on Roman society. Conferring

20. In this section I draw on Rhee, *Loving the Poor, Saving the Rich*, ch. 6.

religious freedom on all, Constantine restored church properties and granted the churches and bishops financial subsidy and clerical exemption from all compulsory public services and personal taxes.[21] With further "pro-Christian" policies before and after his sole reign of the Empire in 324, their overall impact on the church was nothing less than revolutionary. Among other things, he exempted church lands and other properties from pious endowments and taxation, endowed lands in many parts of the Empire, and in sum provided the church with "the abundance of good things" (Eusebius, *Hist. eccl.* 10.8.1). Furthermore, Constantine granted bishops the final judicial authority in arbitrating civil suits especially on behalf of the poor.

With imperial largesse (restricted to the Catholic Church),[22] Constantine made the church not only officially visible but also accountable to the public for the very public gifts it received. Up to this point, the church received offerings from the faithful, especially the middling group and the wealthy, because it primarily cared for the poor of its own, that is, Christians. Now, traditional Christian charity came to be regarded as a public service, and Christian identity was all the more linked to the church's care of the poor in Roman society, both Christians and non-Christians, as "the rich must assume the secular obligations and the poor must be supported by the wealth of the churches" (*Cod. Theod.* 16.2.6). With a Christian population reaching a majority in the mid-fourth century and Christianity becoming a major social force, the church would literally act as a mediator between the rich and the poor of the society, and bishops emerged as "the lovers of the poor" and "the governors of the poor" in their public role.[23]

---

21. These measures only reflected his extension of the privileges that the official religion of the empire enjoyed to Christian churches, although from church's point of view, they still meant a radical change of status, wealth, and privilege.
22. The Catholic Church here refers to the universal, orthodox church as opposed to any sectarian/schismatic (e.g., Donatist) or heretical (e.g., Arian) churches.
23. Cf. P. Brown, *Poverty and Leadership in the Later Roman Empire* (Hanover, NH: University Press of New England, 2002), 32, 45; P. Brown, *Through an Eye of a Needle: Wealth, the Fall of Rome, and the Making of Christianity in the West, 350–550 AD* (Princeton and Oxford: Princeton University Press, 2012), 43–44.

For all the imperial gifts and privileges in exchange for the ecclesiastical care of the poor, the faithful were not necessarily off the hook for their obligation to almsgiving and charity. Although there was hardly a new theological basis of almsgiving that had not already been addressed, church leaders, to be seen in the rest of the readings, tirelessly exhorted the (wealthy) faithful to almsgiving and charity with further theological augmentation. Familiar and interconnected themes continued to appear in the writings of the Greek, Latin, and Syriac Fathers now as the established church tradition: for instance, earthly wealth versus heavenly wealth; almsgiving as effecting atonement for sin and pious lending to God; the symbiotic exchange between the rich and the poor; the pious poor and the wicked rich; God's creative intent of common use for humanity; and identification of the poor with Christ. The last theme underwent significant development in this period; based on Matthew 25:31–45, a classic message now with universal application would be set for the rest of Christian history: in *every* poor person (regardless of one's Christian faith), Christ is fed, given drink, and welcomed as a guest. Whatever is given to the poor is given to Christ. Moreover, condemnation of usury (i.e., lending with interest) became almost universal in this period.

Finally, the Constantinian revolution not only brought about a new era of peace, privilege, and responsibility for the church but also ushered in (organized) monastic movements against the backdrop of imperial Christianity. With the unprecedented development and popularity of the monastic lifestyle and movement, a new group of "the poor" emerged: the ascetics, who practiced voluntary poverty by renouncing private property (as well as social and familial ties) and/or sharing possessions in common with monastic colleagues in communities. The ascetics had been already regarded as "spiritual elites" and "divine men" in the second and third centuries, as shown in the *Acts of Thomas*; but they constituted a "new" formidable Christian elite in the new environment who came to be both entitled to alms and dispensers of alms in complement and competition with the clergy at times. From the mid-fourth century on, an increasing number of bishops (e.g., the Cappadocian Fathers, Ambrose, Augustine, John Chrysostom, and Rabbula) would have experienced monastic life and come from the monastic ranks, thus leading to greater cooperation between clergy/church and monks/monasteries. Some of the ascetics, increasingly coming from aristocratic backgrounds especially in the West (and even Egypt), still maintained their financial independence and civic standings while having "renounced" possessions. A number of the church fathers kept close correspondences with these wealthy aristocratic ascetics, especially females, exhorting and affirming their ascetic lifestyle with generous almsgiving befitting their social status. All the authors selected for this period—the bishops with rhetorical and theological acumen and ascetic/monastic experience—synthesize Greco-Roman civic beneficence and Christian tradition of the care of the poor and reveal the established public role of the bishops as the "lovers and governors of the poor."

Basil the Great

Basil (c. 330–379 CE) was born of an aristocratic Christian family in Cappadocia (modern central Turkey) prominent for its piety, wealth, and social status. He received the best education of the time in Caesarea, Constantinople, and Athens. Shortly after beginning his career as a rhetorician, however, he received baptism, sold his possessions, and distributed the proceeds to the poor, following Matthew 19:21. He then visited various monastic communities in Palestine, Syria, and Egypt and founded communal ("cenobitic") monastic communities across Cappadocia, for which he wrote extensive instructions, known as the *Longer Rules* and the *Shorter Rules*. He was ordained a priest in Caesarea, the capital of Cappadocia, in 363 and then bishop of Caesarea and metropolitan of Cappadocia in 370. He proved himself to be a skillful church leader and administrator in dealing with many political and ecclesiastical negotiations, an astute theologian in advocating the Trinitarian doctrine and the Nicene position against (neo-)Arian heresy, a powerful preacher, and an effective social activist on behalf of the poor. Basil built his famous hospital/hospice just outside Caesarea around 372; Basil's "New City" (as it was called by Gregory of Nazianzus) housed strangers, the poor, the sick, and the elderly as well as lepers and the mutilated, many of whom needed medical treatments and care (Basil, *Letter* 94; Gregory, *Oration* 43.63). Two of his brothers (Peter and Gregory) also became bishops, and his eldest sister, Macrina, renowned for her ascetic piety, was profoundly influential on Basil and his younger brother Gregory, bishop of Nyssa.

Basil, his brother Gregory of Nyssa, and his friend Gregory of Nazianzus are collectively known as the Cappadocian Fathers. They not only brought the rich heritage of classical Greek philosophy and literature to bear upon their work as Christian pastors, theologians, teachers, and writers but also shared a deep commitment to the poor and the afflicted and to distributive justice.

In 368, a catastrophic drought and famine, mentioned by all three, struck Caesarea and its surrounding area, resulting in massive crop failures and a severe food shortage throughout the region. Basil's selected homilies were all delivered around the time of famine. In *Homily 6: "I Will Pull Down My Barns"* (c. 369), Basil displays his homiletic efforts to open the local granaries during the famine as a part of institutional relief. In preaching about the story of the foolish rich man who said "I will pull down my barns" to build larger ones rather than to consider his own mortality [Luke 12:1–12], Basil describes the poor as the victims of injustice and addresses his audience as the rich who willfully deprive the poor of grain, intent to make a profit while taking from the poor whatever they have. In this context, he provides the most vivid image of the poor man who must sell his beloved children in the slave market to feed the rest of his family. For Basil, the poor are agents of God's justice against the rich who refuse to offer their wealth to alleviate suffering.

In *Homily 7: To the Rich*, Basil deals with the familiar text of Jesus's dialogue with the rich young man in Matthew 19:16–22. While Clement of Alexandria saw the spiritual problem of the rich young man more as his attachment to worldly riches, Basil sees it more as his violation of the commandment of loving his neighbor as himself (1). Basil represents a change of attitude in the post-Constantinian context in that he understands the story in primarily social rather than individual terms, even for redemptive almsgiving. Therefore, explaining the failure of the crops and famine in *Homily 8: In Time of Famine and Drought*, he defines them in terms of human sin that causes nature to act against its nature. As in Lactantius, God's natural created world is a model of justice, kindness, and generosity, which should be imitated by all—the rich in particular—in sharp contrast to the prevailing civil disorder. Thus, Basil equates not sharing surplus possessions with committing murder as he highlights humanity of the poor as natural kin. His *Homily on Psalm 14: Against Lending with Interest*, then delves into the inhumanity of lending at interest to the poor (and the rich) as it forces them into debt and enslavement as a social disease. These texts, along with the selected *Shorter Rule*, accentuate the social purpose and function of riches and advocate (the monastic ideal of) sufficiency, simplicity, and communal distribution of wealth as Christian civic ideal.

Gregory of Nyssa

The younger brother of Basil, Gregory (c. 335–394 CE) also received a fine education in Cappadocia and became a rhetorician. He was appointed bishop of Nyssa by Basil in 372 and served in that post until death. With Gregory of Nazianzus, Gregory joined Basil in defending Nicene orthodoxy and articulating what would become the classic Trinitarian doctrine with the divinity of the Holy Spirit, which was ratified at the second ecumenical council, the Council of Constantinople, in 381. He was committed to church unity and was the most mystical and contemplative theologian among the Cappadocian Fathers.

Gregory wrote two sermons titled *On the Love of the Poor*, the second of which (along with Gregory of Nazianzus's sermon on the same theme) offers one of the most extensive descriptions and Christian images of leprosy and the lepers in their physical agony as the worthy objects of Christian philanthropy. In his first sermon *On the Love of the Poor*, which is our selected text, he describes the destitute in general and emphasizes again their dignity, sharing the image of God. This common humanity as natural kin warrants common and equal sharing of resources with one another against one's exclusive or absolute ownership. Therefore, those who fast for spiritual discipline should recognize its social function as a means of justice, as mandated in Isaiah 58. As with Basil and Gregory of Nazianzus, Gregory of Nyssa makes the poor visible in Christian civic society as powerful agents to effect redemptive almsgiving.

Gregory of Nazianzus

Gregory (c. 329–390 CE) was born to wealthy, landed parents, trained in rhetoric and philosophy with Basil in Athens, and sought a contemplative life as a devoted monk. Against his will, Gregory was first ordained a priest by his father (who was then bishop of Nazianzus) in 361 and then bishop of Sasima (again against his will) by his best friend, Basil, in 372. This caused a rift in their friendship, which took a significant time to heal. He became the bishop of Constantinople in 380 and presided over the first part of the Council of Constantinople in 381. Called "the Christian Demosthenes" because of the power of his oratory and "the Theologian" in the Greek tradition, Gregory's orations, poems, and letters reveal his meticulous care for theological terminology, rhetoric, and classical education for the life of the church.

His *Oration 14: On the Love of the Poor* is a fine example of that. As with Basil and Gregory of Nyssa, Gregory Nazianzen maximizes the force of classical rhetoric by making a moving appeal to love the poor, especially the lepers, in imitation of God's love of humanity (*philanthrōpia*) and to serve God (Christ) in the poor. As with his friends, Gregory defends the "human rights" of the poor and the lepers for relief and justice based on a shared human nature and shared divine image. Here, even more than his friends, Gregory fully identifies the body of the poor, including the lepers, with that of Christ; their suffering bodies are connected to the incarnate body of Christ and thus are to elicit appropriate emotions and actions from the audience.

This oration and the two sermons by Gregory of Nyssa were likely written in support of Basil's efforts to organize relief and care for the poor and the sick, which culminated in the construction of his hospital around 372.

John Chrysostom

We now meet one of the most celebrated preachers of (early) Christianity, John, known as Chrysostom, "Golden Mouth," in Antioch, Syria. Antioch's wealth, status, and ecclesiastical prominence rivaled the other leading metropolises of the Empire: Rome, Alexandria, and Constantinople. Younger contemporary of the Cappadocian Fathers, John (c. 349–407 CE) was born to faithful Christian parents and educated under Libanius, the famous pagan rhetorician. After his education, as with the Cappadocians and other devout people of the day, John joined monastic seclusion for some time. He was ordained a priest in 386 by Bishop Flavian of Antioch; it was in Antioch where he gained a reputation for his preaching, especially against the materialism and public entertainment of the rank and file. In Antioch, John also led churches to organize major relief efforts for widows, orphans, virgins, beggars, homeless immigrants, the sick, and the poor through church-administered orphanages, hostels, and hospitals. Unexpectedly, however, he was called to Constantinople to be ordained its Patriarch in 398 by the emperor Arcadius. John immediately began to reform the moral and spiritual life of the imperial city, including the court and its clergy, preaching against abuses of wealth and power and public sins such as the theater to the offence of the wealthy and influential citizens of the capital. John practiced his preaching: he not only supported financially the existing hostels and hospitals but established several more, placing them under the control of his trusted clergy and hiring doctors, cooks, and other staff for medical care of the indigent sick. Nevertheless, the combination of his brutal honesty, asceticism, tactlessness, and uncompromising intensity for reform, joined with the enmity of the Patriarch of Alexandria and empress Eudoxia, brought about his downfall. He was deposed from his position in 403, subsequently recalled, and then deposed again by empress Eudoxia and exiled to Armenia and finally to Pontus, where he died in 407.

A prolific writer, Chrysostom left letters and treatises on various topics such as the monastic life, virginity, and priesthood, but most of his works are homilies[24] on the books of the Bible and theological and moral subjects such as repentance, almsgiving, and on Lazarus and the rich man in Luke 16. Our selection of his texts comes from various homilies (mostly from his Antioch period) to show that proper use of wealth and the care of the poor was indeed John's consistent and pervasive concern. Familiar themes such as the "wicked rich" and their duty to distribute any superfluous wealth, the utility and social function of wealth, and the condemnation of usury appear with exegetical force and eloquence. Following the rich tradition, John argues that the essence of riches is its usefulness to the common good and use—the alleviation of the sufferings of the poor of the society. Thus a sin of omission (not sharing or giving alms in proportion to one's wealth) is just as wicked as a sin of commission (robbery or usury); both form a crime of inhumanity as they destroy the human bond of solidarity and interdependence.

As with the Cappadocians, Chrysostom brings the poor into the church and civic space as a witness against the inhumanity and unjust ownership of the rich, whose presence was signif-

---

24. More than nine hundred, although not all are originally by Chrysostom.

icant in his churches in Antioch and Constantinople, and to whom he directed his homilies with such fiery emotion and frustration at times. Hence, although it may seem rather naive to modern readers, Chrysostom seems to have believed in the church's ability to reach the poor if (rich) Christians really lived out the biblical mandate to care for their neighbors through active and sustained almsgiving.

Ambrose of Milan

As we turn to the Latin West, we encounter bishops just as towering and influential as their contemporary Eastern colleagues. Ambrose (c. 339–397 CE), born of an aristocratic Christian family in Gaul (modern France), received a fine classical education befitting his family status (rhetoric, law, and Greek in particular) and had a legal career until he became the provincial governor of Aemilia-Liguria in 370. While still a catechumen (before baptism), and against his will, Ambrose was chosen to be the bishop of Milan in 373 to succeed an Arian bishop. Upon his ordination, Ambrose gave all his property to the church and to the poor. Through his tireless and influential work as a preacher, teacher, and defender of orthodoxy against Arianism, Ambrose elevated Milan (the imperial residence then) to the most important See[25] of the West. Ambrose was a powerful ecclesiastical statesman, advocating for the church's union with the empire while maintaining its independence from the imperial power, especially on moral issues. Ambrose was also instrumental in introducing burgeoning Eastern monasticism into the West. He was later named a Doctor of the Church in the West.

The selected texts come from *On Naboth*, *On Tobit*, *On the Duties of the Clergy*, and his letter to Bishop Constantinus, representing Ambrose's most important works on our topic. In the first two exegetical works, the influence of Basil's *Homilies 6, 7*, and *Homily on Psalm 14: Against Lending with Interest* is evident. In *On Naboth* Ambrose offers a cogent critique against the

---

25. The official seat or jurisdiction, or office, of a bishop.

destructive greed of the rich, based on the account of Naboth's vineyard in 1 Kings 21, and uses the parable of the rich fool in Luke 12 as a commentary on the former. In *On Tobit* Ambrose contends against the unjust practice of usury, drawing heavily on Basil's *Homily on Psalm 14: Against Lending with Interest.* Ambrose's best-known writing, *On the Duties of the Clergy* (*De officiis ministrorum*), is the first treatise on Christian ethics modeled after Cicero's *De officiis.* Offering practical moral guidance to the Milanese clergy, Ambrose follows the Stoic moral precepts but Christianizes them with scriptural understanding.

Ambrose defines justice primarily as a social virtue that secures the common good along with the other cardinal virtues, even as it is dictated by nature (cf. Lactantius). Agreeing with the Greek Fathers, Ambrose believes that the earth and its resources are the common property of humankind in the sense that all human beings have a "natural right" to make use of them; private ownership is always contingent and limited in its use for the common good, particularly for the poor, and also for the good of the possessor's soul. As with his Greek colleagues, Ambrose regards private ownership/property in absolute and exclusive forms as the result of sin and greed, the opposite of the (post-)Enlightenment claim of private ownership/property as a "natural," inviolate, and divine right.

Augustine of Hippo

Augustine (354–430 CE), also a Doctor of the Church in the West, is considered by far the most extraordinary Latin theologian in early Christianity and beyond. He was born in Thagaste in North Africa; his father was a town councilor of modest means, and his mother, Monica, was a Christian. His father managed, even beyond his means, to obtain a first-class education for Augustine in the hope that the family would advance in the social and economic ladder through the successful career of their gifted son. Indeed, as a result of this elite education, Augustine taught rhetoric in Carthage, Rome, and Milan, where he converted to Christianity and received baptism by

Ambrose in 387. Once a member of the Manichaean religion for ten years, Augustine learned a form of Christianity interpreted in Neo-Platonic terms by Ambrose. Having lived the typically unchaste life of a Roman of his social standing for a long time, Augustine embraced a life of chastity and cenobitic monasticism after his conversion and baptism and gave up his personal property for the poor (in stages). On a visit to Hippo Regius, Augustine was unexpectedly ordained a priest against his will in 391. He served as the bishop of the city from 395/6 until his death in 430, while Hippo was under siege by the Vandals.

As the Greek Fathers brought together Christian, Platonic, and Greco-Roman traditions for Eastern theology and the Greek-speaking churches, so Augustine synthesized Christian, Platonic, and Latin Roman traditions in a most unique way for the Western churches and theology with enduring legacy. Many of his voluminous writings were occasioned by, or were written in the midst of, the many controversies in which he participated throughout his life. These included controversies with Manichaeism, Donatism, Pelagianism, and paganism. Of his works, the *Confessions*, *On the Trinity*, and the *City of God* remain the most famous to this day.

Augustine's teaching on wealth and poverty is scattered in his writings and is rooted in his fundamental distinction between "use" (*uti*) and "enjoyment" (*frui*), as he shows in *On Christian Doctrine*. Wealth is to be only a means (*uti*) to obtain the true object of our desire (*frui*—e.g., eternal life, eternal happiness, ultimately God) in the hierarchy of goods, not the other way around. Virtue consists in enjoying (*frui*) proper objects of love for their sake and using (*uti*) proper objects of instrument well without loving them, whereas vice involves mixing up and reversing the order. In the three selected letters, Augustine probes this distinction further as well as the relationship between possessions and possessors. In classical Greco-Roman understanding, the rich person, the person with possessions and status, was considered to be the good person, the virtuous one; the one without possessions or social status was, therefore, considered to be not virtuous. Augustine inverts the paradigm. People do not become virtuous by their possessions, but the goods (e.g., riches, positions, honor, etc.) become good in the hands of the virtuous only as the latter make good use of the former for the sake of the true (heavenly) life (*Letter* 130). Conversely, the use of goods in a bad way is the wrongful use of goods and as such deprives the possessor of his or her "right" of ownership (*Letter* 153).

Augustine applies this thinking in a most ingenious way in the selected *Tractates* in his debate with the Donatists, a North African schismatic group who claimed to have legitimate ownership of their churches. While acknowledging that their claim could be justified either by Scripture or human law (i.e., the imperial laws), Augustine argues that the first option is ruled out, since Scripture does not specify the ownership in the concrete situation. If the Donatists resort to the human laws, their argument is self-defeating as the imperial laws deny their right of ownership because of their illegitimacy—that is, they are "heretics," having separated themselves from the Catholic Church. In either case, argues Augustine, the Donatists have no legitimate claim.

Augustine expounds on the rich, salvation, and riches in his Letter to Hilarius (*Letter* 157), who had raised a concern on whether the rich could be saved without total renunciation. The Pelagians (followers of Pelagius, another contemporary influential theologian and rival of Augustine) had answered negatively. Coming back to the same issue addressed by Clement of Alexandria, Augustine argues that the righteous rich are such by virtue of their proper use of wealth through works of charity. To do so, Augustine first debunks the twin argument of the inherent goodness of poverty and the inherent evil of wealth and then turns to the apostle Paul's encouragement to the rich in 1 Timothy 6. At the same time, Augustine affirms Jesus's command to the rich young man (Matthew 19; Mark 10; Luke 18), first by distinguishing the "commandments of the law and that of higher perfection" (25) and then by internalizing the rich man's problem as his pride and attachment. Harmonizing Paul's counsel and the Lord's precept, Augustine supports a "two-tiered" approach where he can approve both the ascetic/monastic poor on the road to perfection and "the weaker souls" (i.e., the righteous rich) who still put "their hope not in the uncertainty of riches, but in the living God" (33).[26] In his *Exposition on Psalm 38* and two sermons, Augustine follows a rich tradition as he argues against the accumulation of wealth beyond necessities (i.e., superfluidity) and usury for its social obligation and advocates for generous almsgiving to the poor (through the church) for the benefit of both the rich and the poor.

Compared to the Eastern Fathers, Augustine's understanding of wealth and admonitions to the rich display a "softer tone" and resemble more of Clement of Alexandria in that he regarded wealth as a providential reality of life. Augustine was not as concerned with the acquisition of wealth as he was with its use. Furthermore, Augustine's perspective was conditioned by his controversies with Manichees, Donatists, and Pelagians, who all tended to be much more rigorous in their ascetic ideals and practices—even as he continued to care for widows, orphans, and the poor, and shared many traditional themes.

Leo the Great

Leo the Great (d. 461 CE) was one of the most outstanding popes of Christian antiquity (the first of only two popes to bear the title "the Great") and set a path for the papacy in the early medieval period with his ecclesiastical, doctrinal, and political roles. Leo was mentioned by Augustine in a letter (*Letter* 19); in 418, as a young acolyte, Leo delivered to the bishop of Carthage the letter of Pope Zosimus about the Pelagian heresy. As archdeacon, Leo was sent on many ecclesiastical and civil diplomatic missions and was unanimously elected to serve as pope in 440, which he did until his death in 461. As

---

26. Later, this "two-tiered" approach will be made formal in the West by the official distinction between "precepts" (obligatory commandments for all) and "counsels" (higher exhortations for those who pursue perfection, i.e., monastics).

the Western Roman empire was experiencing prolonged disintegration and upheaval from the migrations and invasions of Germanic tribes, Leo expanded the papal claim of "the Chair of St. Peter" beyond the West, sought to unify the church against heretics (e.g., Manichees, Pelagianism, and Eutychianim), and exercised influence on the Council of Chalcedon (451) with his *Tome*. Leo stood for Christianized Roman civilization and culture as he negotiated peace with Attila the Hun (452) and Gaiseric the Vandal (455) and sought to preserve civil stability in the West.

In the mid-440s Leo instituted a special collection for the poor as a united effort by the Christians in the city of Rome intended to counter an ostentatious pagan festival.[27] This provides a context for his selected sermons. Leo followed Augustine in his basic orientation to wealth and accepted it as God's good gift not to be shunned but to be used and managed well on behalf of the poor, through the church, to the spiritual interest of the possessor. Leo argues for a priority of almsgiving that trumps but also benefits all other virtues, drawing on the well-known notion of "Christ in the poor" in Matthew 25; the call to alms is not just for the rich but for everyone, since everyone is subject to its reward as well as its judgment (due to its lack). Instead of practicing "evil usury," the congregation should practice "holy usury" (i.e., almsgiving). In contrast to the Eastern Fathers, there is no sense in his sermons that the city was filled with large crowds of the destitute; rather, Leo's poor are seen as the impoverished aristocrats and citizens covered by the church's care of the poor. Thus, in his changing context, Leo encourages his congregation to see the poor as "brothers"—the entire community of citizens entitled to care in times of suffering, as already evidenced in Ambrose.

Rabbula of Edessa

We finally come back to Syria with Rabbula, bishop of Edessa

---

27. See Brown, *Through the Eye of a Needle*, 465–68. I draw on some of Brown's analyses of Leo's sermons in this paragraph.

from 412 to 436 CE. Rabbula was born into a wealthy elite family living near Qenneshrin, some ninety kilometers southeast of Antioch. His father was a pagan priest, his mother was a Christian, and they gave their son a fine education in Greek. His conversion was occasioned by his witnessing a miraculous healing by a Christian hermit, Abraham, in one of his estates. Rabbula sold his estates and possessions, distributed all he had to the poor, and took up a strict life of asceticism and solitude. He was ordained a bishop in 412, and his episcopacy was marked by his zealous promotion of Christianity against paganism, continuing asceticism, sacrificial ministry to and care for the poor and the sick and the whole city, and an ardent fight against heretics. Rabbula was involved with one of the greatest theological controversies of his time concerning the union of divine and human natures in Christ, which was represented in the doctrinal, ecclesiastical, and personal disputes between Cyril, bishop of Alexandria, and Nestorius, bishop of Constantinople. Rabbula supported the hypostatic union of Cyril, the winner of the third ecumenical council, the Council of Ephesus (431), against Nestorius, who was condemned and exiled. Rabbula also supported the Formula of Union (433), which attempted to unite the Christian factions in the East, following the Council of Ephesus.

Our main source for his life and episcopal ministry is the Syriac *Life of Rabbula*, from which our text comes. Praised as one of the most excellent works of Syriac biography, the *Life* portrays Rabbula as an ideal and model bishop for his clergy and flock. Its particular focus is his almsgiving to the poor and the sick and his ascetic lifestyle. Our selection starts with his distribution of his possessions to the poor following his conversion and embrace of an austere life of asceticism after he was relieved of all his responsibilities as *paterfamilias* (the head of household). As an ascetic bishop, Rabbula not only gives all his wealth, but channels all the private contributions to and accumulated wealth of the church in Edessa to support widows, orphans, the poor, and the sick. Rabbula argued that Christians ought to give away their surplus, living on only what is necessary in life; whatever the church receives from these faithful should be used to provide for the needs of the poor. His love of the poor is highlighted by restoring the hospital for the men and building one for the women of the city. Though idealized, the *Life* shows Rabbula in action, in actual engagement and interactions with the poor, as their patron—praying for them, caring for them, and comforting them through his touch, especially the lepers. This is how the church serves the welfare of the city. Rabbula may be compared to the Cappadocian Fathers and John Chrysostom for his "love of the poor."

1

The Shepherd of Hermas

Visions[1]

14 (3.6). "And do you want to know who are the ones that are broken in pieces and thrown far away from the tower? These are the children of lawlessness; they believed hypocritically, and no wickedness escaped them. Therefore they do not have salvation, because they are not useful for building on account of their wickedness. This is why they were broken up and thrown far away, because of the Lord's wrath, for they angered him. As for the others you saw lying around in great numbers and not going into the building, the ones that are damaged are those who have known the truth but did not abide in it, nor do they associate with the saints. Therefore they are useless." "But who are the ones with cracks?" "These are the ones who have something against one another in their hearts and are not at peace among themselves. Instead, they

---

1. Translation of the texts come from Michael W. Holmes, *The Apostolic Fathers: Greek Texts and English Translations* (3rd ed.; Grand Rapids: Baker Academic, 2007). Used by permission.

have only the appearance of peace, and when they leave one another their evil thoughts remain in their hearts. These are the cracks that the stones have. . . ." "And who are the white and round stones that do not fit into the building, Lady?"[2] She answered and said to me, "How long will you be foolish and stupid, asking about everything and understanding nothing? Theses are the ones who have faith, but also have riches of this world. Whenever persecution comes, they deny their Lord because of their riches and their business affairs." And I answered her and said, "Then when, Lady, will they be useful for the building?" "When," she replied, "their riches, which lead their souls astray, are cut away, then they will be useful to God. For just as the round stone cannot become square unless it is trimmed and loses some part of itself, so also with those who are rich in this world cannot become useful to the Lord unless their riches are cut away. Learn first from yourself: when you were rich, you were useless, but now you are useful and beneficial to life. Be useful to God, for you yourself are to be used as one of these stones."

17 (3.9). "Listen, my[3] children. I brought you up in much sincerity and innocence, and reverence through the mercy of the Lord, who instilled righteousness in you in order that you may be justified and sanctified from all perversity. Yet you do not want to cease from your wickedness. Now listen to me and be at peace among yourselves, and be concerned for one another and assist one another; and do not partake of God's creation in abundance by yourselves, but also share with those in need. For by overeating some people bring on themselves fleshly weaknesses and injure their flesh, while the flesh of those who do not have anything to eat is injured because they do not have enough food, and their bodies are wasting away. This lack of community spirit is harmful to those of you who have, yet do not share with those in need. Look to the coming judgment. You, therefore, who have more than enough, seek out those who are hungry, until the tower is finished. For after the tower

---

2. The elderly woman, Hermas's revelatory guide, representing the church.
3. The same "Lady."

is finished, you may want to do good, but you will have not the chance. Beware, therefore, you who exult in your wealth, lest those in need groan, and their groaning rise up to the Lord, and you together with your good things be shut outside the door of the tower. Now, therefore, I say to you who lead the church and occupy the seats of honor: do not be like the sorcerers. For the sorcerers carry their drugs in bottles, but you carry your drug and poison in the heart. You are calloused and do not want to cleanse your hearts and to mix your wisdom together in a clean heart, in order that you may receive mercy from the great King. Watch out, therefore, children, these divisions of yours deprive you of your life. How is it that you desire to instruct God's elect, while you yourselves have no instruction? Instruct one another, therefore, and have peace among yourselves, in order that I too may stand joyfully before the Father and give an account on behalf of all of you to your Lord."

Parables

50 (1). He[4] spoke to me, "You know," he said, "that you who are servants of God are living in a foreign country, for your city is far from this city. If, therefore, you know," he said, "your city in which you are destined to live, why do you prepare fields and expensive possessions and buildings and useless rooms here? If you are preparing these things for this city, you obviously are not planning to return to your own city. Foolish and double-minded and miserable person, do you not realize that all these things are foreign to you, and under someone else's authority? For the lord of this city will say, 'I do not want you to live in my city; instead, leave this city, because you do not conform to my laws.' So, you who have fields and dwellings and many other possessions, what will you do with your field and your house and all the other things you have prepared for yourself when you are expelled by him? For the lord of this country has every right to say to you, 'Either conform to my

---

4. The Shepherd, the angel set over repentance, who becomes Hermas's new revelatory guide, interpreter, and instructor.

WEALTH AND POVERTY IN EARLY CHRISTIANITY

laws, or get out of my country.' So what are you going to do, since you are subject to the law of your own city? For the sake of your fields and the rest of your possessions, will you totally renounce your own law and live according to the law of this city? Take are; it may not be in your best interest to renounce your law, for if you should want to return to your city, you will certainly not be accepted, because you have renounced the law of your city, and will be shut out of it. So take care; as one living in a foreign land, do not prepare for yourself one thing more than is necessary to be self-sufficient, and be prepared so that whenever the master of this city wants to expel you because of you opposition to his law, you can leave his city and come to your own city, and joyfully conform to your law, free from all insult. Take care, therefore, that you serve the Lord and have him in your heart; do God's works, remembering his commandments and the promises that he made, and trust him to keep them, if his commandments are kept. So instead of fields, buy souls that are in distress, as anyone is able, and visit widows and orphans, and do not neglect them; and spend your wealth and all your possessions, which you received from God, on fields and houses of this kind. For this is why the Master made you rich, so that you might perform these ministries for him. It is much better to purchase fields and possessions and houses of this kind, which you will find in your own city when you go home to it. This lavish expenditure is beautiful and joyous; it does not bring grief or fear, but joy. So do not practice the extravagance of the outsiders, for it is unprofitable to you, the servants of God. But do practice your own extravagance, in which you can rejoice; and do not imitate or touch what belongs to another or covet it, for it is evil to covet someone else's things. But do your own task, and you will be saved."

51 (2). As I was walking in the country, I noticed an elm tree and a vine and was comparing them and their fruits when the shepherd appeared to me and said, "What are you thinking about?" "I am thinking, sir," I said, "about the elm and the vine; specifically, that they are very well suited to one another." "These two trees," he said, "are intended as a model for God's

4

servants." "Sir," I said, "I would like to know the model represented by these trees of which you speak." "Do you see," he asked, "the elm and the vine?" "I see them, sir," I replied. "This vine," he said, "bears fruit, but the elm is a fruitless tree. But unless it climbs the elm, this vine cannot bear much fruit when it is spread out on the ground, and what fruit it does bear is rotten, because it is not suspended from the elm. So, when the vine is attached to the elm it bears fruit both from itself and from the elm. You see, therefore, that the elm also bears much fruit, not less than the vine, but even more." "How, sir," I asked, "does it bear more?" "Because," he said, "the vine, when hanging on the elm, bears its fruit in abundance and in good condition; but when it is spread out on the ground, it bears little fruit, and what it does bear is rotten. So this parable is applicable to God's servants, to poor and rich alike." "How so, sir?" I asked. "Explain this to me." "Listen," he said. "The rich have much wealth, but are poor in the things of the Lord, being distracted by their wealth, and they have very little confession and prayer with the Lord, and what they do have is small and weak and has no power above. So whenever the rich go up to the poor and supply them their needs, they believe that what they do for the poor will be able to find a reward from God, because the poor are rich intercession and confession, and their intercession has great power with God. The rich, therefore, unhesitatingly provide the poor with everything. And the poor, being provided for by the rich, pray for them, thanking God for those who share with them. And the rich in turn are all the more zealous on behalf of the poor, in order that they may lack nothing in their life, for the rich know that the intercession of the poor is acceptable and rich before God. They both, then, complete their work: the poor work with prayer, in which they are rich, which they received from the Lord; this they return to the Lord who supplies them with it. And the rich likewise unhesitatingly share with the poor the wealth that they received from the Lord. And this work is great and acceptable to God, because the rich understand about their wealth and work for the poor by using the gifts of the Lord, and cor-

5

rectly fulfill their ministry. So, as far as people are concerned, the elm does not seem to bear fruit, and they neither know nor realize that if a drought comes the elm, which has water, nourishes the vine, and the vine, having a constant supply of water, bears double the fruit, both for itself and for the elm. So also the poor, by appealing to the Lord on behalf of the rich, complement their wealth, and again, the rich, by providing for the needs of the poor, complement their souls. So, then, both become partners in the righteous work. Therefore, the one who does these things will not be abandoned by God, but will be enrolled in the books of the living. Blessed are the rich who also understand that they have been made rich by the Lord, for the one who comprehends this will be able to do some good work."

2

Clement of Alexandria

The Rich Man's Salvation[1]

1. Those who make flattering speeches in order to impress the rich are, it seems to me, showoffs and victims of their own low self-esteem, for they attempt to gain recognition by praising things that are valueless. Such people are also blasphemous and deceitful. They are blasphemous because they do not praise and glorify God, from whom and in whom all things exist, but rather they give this glory due God to people who wallow in filthy and despicable lives. For this reason they will face God's judgment. They are deceitful because they encourage the rich to delude themselves by showering them with false praise, which causes them to focus even more on their wealth and the admiration it arouses. The rich are already in danger of being corrupted by self-pride without such deceitful influence. As the proverb says, they are adding "fire to fire"[2]

---

1. Translation of this text, except pars. 19, 31, 32, comes from Jan L. Womer, ed. and trans., *Morality and Ethics in Early Christianity* (Sources of Early Christian Thought; Philadelphia: Fortress, 1987).

or "pride to pride" and arrogance to the pressures that wealth brings. It would be better if wealth were downplayed and even diminished, for it is a dangerous and deadly disease. The one who exalts and exaggerates oneself is in danger of losing everything, as the divine Word declares. It seems to me that we do better if we try to help the wealthy to work out their salvation in every possible way rather than to praise and encourage them in what is harmful to them. First, we should pray that God will grant salvation to the rich, for we know that he will gladly answer our prayer. Then, with the Savior's grace to heal their souls, we should teach them and lead them to the truth. Only those who reach the truth and are distinguished by good works will gain the prize of eternal life. Prayer requires a life that is well disciplined and persevering until the last day of life, and our life of discipline demands a good and committed attitude that seeks always to follow the Lord's commands.

2. The reason why salvation seems more difficult for the rich than for the poor is complicated. Some people, by only causally hearing the words of the Lord about its being easier for a camel to pass through the eye of a needle than for a wealthy person to enter the kingdom of heaven, suddenly take a look at themselves and see that they are not destined for salvation. They give up in despair and become completely a part of this world, with no concern for the world to come and no interest in the teachings of our Teacher and Master and his description of who the rich really are or how God makes possible what seems impossible to humans. On the other hand, others understand this saying rightly and properly, but they fail to see the importance of works that lead to salvation, and therefore they do not amend their lives as is necessary for those who have this hope. In both cases I am referring to the wealthy who have already learned about the Savior's power and his glorious salvation. I am not concerned with those who have not yet come to understand this truth.

3. It is the duty of all who love truth and who are a part of the Christian community not to treat wealthy members of

---

2. A common Greek proverb.

the church with rude contempt or, on the other hand, to bow to them in order to benefit from their friendship and generosity. Use the words of Scripture to help them overcome their despair, and show them with interpretation of the Lord's teachings that the kingdom of heaven is not an impossible goal for them if they will obey the commandments. After that, you should help them to understand that their fears are groundless, for the Savior will gladly receive them if they so desire. Teach them what kind of works and attitudes they need in order to reach their hoped goal. It is a goal within their grasp, but it will require effort! If you will allow me an analogy that compares the insignificant and perishable with the great and imperishable, I would see the rich as athletes. One of them sees no hope to win but is unwilling to train, exercise, and eat properly, and so fails to gain the prize. The person invested with wealth should not feel that he [or she] is already excluded from the Lord's prizes. Remain faithful and look at the greatness of God's love toward all people! But do not expect to reach the goal without discipline and effort, and without training and perseverance. Let the Word become your trainer and allow Christ to be the referee of the contest; let the food and drink of the Lord's new covenant become your nourishment; let the commandments prescribe your exercises. Your life should be richly decorated with the virtues of love, faith, hope, knowledge of the truth, compassion, gentleness, humility, and seriousness, so that when the last trumpet sounds to signal the end of the race and our departure from this life, you may stand before the judge with a good conscience as the victor [cf. 1 Cor 9:24–25]. The judge shall admit you as one worthy of entering the heavenly kingdom, where you will receive the victor's crown amid the acclamations of the angels.

4. May the Savior grant me guidance as I continue my teaching from this point so that I will offer advice that is true, appropriate, and helpful for your salvation. First, I want to discuss the meaning of hope itself, and, second, to help you see how you reach such hope. The Lord gives freely to those in need; he gives understanding to those who ask and dispels their igno-

rance and despair. His words are repeated again and again so that the wealthy may become interpreters for themselves and understand the words fully. There is nothing better than to listen again to what we have heard before from the gospel. Do not let them depress you as they did when you listened with the uncritical and mistaken logic of immature understanding.

> As he went on his way, a man came and knelt before him, asking, "Good teacher, what must I do to inherit eternal life?" Jesus said, "Why do you call me good? No one is good except God. You know the commandments: do not commit adultery; do not kill; do not steal; do not give false testimony; honor your father and mother." The man answered, "I have done all of these things, since I was young." Jesus looked at him with love and replied, "You lack one thing. If you want to be perfect,[3] sell all that you possess and give it to the poor, and you will have valuable possessions in heaven. Then come and follow me." His countenance fell immediately, and he went away dejected, for he had great possessions. Jesus looked around and then said to his disciples, "How difficult it will be for those who heave wealth to enter the kingdom of God!" The disciples were startled at his words. Jesus said to them, "Children, how difficult it is for those who put their trust in riches to enter the kingdom of God! It would be easier for a camel to move through the eye of a needle than for a rich person to enter the kingdom of God." The disciples were greatly dismayed and asked, "Who then can be saved?" He said to them, "With men it is impossible, but not with God." Peter said to him, "We have left everything we had to follow you." Jesus answered, "In truth I say to you, whoever leaves home and parents, brothers and possessions for my sake and the cause of the gospel will receive a hundredfold; in this life, houses and lands, possessions, brothers, sisters, and persecutions; in the time to come, eternal life. The first will be last, and the last first." [Mark 10:17–31]

9. Jesus does not accuse the man of having failed to fulfill the law. Instead, he loves him and warmly commends him for his faithfulness. However, the man is not perfect as regards eter-

---

3. This crucial part is a Matthean variation (Matt 19:21) in the established edition. The text of the Gospel of Mark used by Clement had differences in some aspects from the contemporary version.

nal life, inasmuch as he did not fulfill what is perfect; and while he indeed obeys the law, he does not understand the truelife. Who would deny that works of the law are good? The "commandment is holy" [Rom 7:12] inasmuch as it provides training that is regulated by fear and preparatory discipline. This will lead to the culmination of legalism and the emergence of the grace of Jesus [Gal 3:24]. Christ is the fulfillment of the law and in him all who believe are justified [Rom 10:4]. Those who do the Father's work are not turned into slaves but are made his sons and daughters and joint-heirs.

10. "If you want to be perfect"—by this Jesus implied that he was not yet perfect, for there are no intermediate categories. "If you want" is a divine affirmation of the free will that the rich man possessed. The decision was his, but the gift was God's. God freely gives this gift of salvation to those who ask for it in sincerity. God does not force it upon us, for he hates the use of force, but he provides for those who seek, and he gives to those who ask and to those who seek, and he gives to those who ask and to those who knock [Matt 7:7; Luke 11:9]. If this is your desire, if it is your honest wish and not a bit of self-deception, you may take what is offered. "You lack one thing," the thing that Christ offers, the good that is above the law and that the law cannot give because it does not possess it. This good is only for those who live in Christ. The man who had lived by the law from his youth and was proud of this accomplishment could not accomplish the one task the Savior gave him in order to reach the eternal life that he desired. He went away dejected, realizing he could not fulfill the requirement that separated him from the life he had requested. His interest was not in eternal life, as he had said, but in the desire to merely gain respect for good intentions. There were many things he could do with his goal, but he lacked strength and dedication to accomplish the work that would give him life. We also see this when the Savior spoke to Martha, who was busy with many things, preoccupied and distracted with entertaining, and annoyed that he sister sat and listened to Jesus rather than helping with the tasks at hand: "You are troubled with many things, but Mary

has chosen a better option and it will be of lasting benefit to her" [Luke 10:38–42]. The Lord asked the rich man to give up his many activities and to concentrate on the one that brought the grace of him who offered eternal life.

11. What was it that caused the man to run away and to reject his teacher his inquiry, his hope, his goal, and his life of obedience? "Sell all that you possess": what does this mean? It does not mean, as some superficially suppose, that he should throw away all that he owns and abandon his property. Rather, he is to banish those attitudes toward wealth that permeate his whole life, his desires, interests, and anxiety. These things become the thorns choking the seed of a true life [cf. Mark 4:19]. It is not a great thing or desirable to be without any wealth, unless it is because we are seeking eternal life. If it were, those who possess nothing—the destitute, the beggars seeking food, and the poor living in the streets—would become the blessed and loved of God, even though they did not know God or God's righteousness. They would be grated eternal life on the basis of their extreme poverty and their lack of even the basic necessities of life! The renunciation of wealth and the distribution of possessions to the poor are nothing new. Even before the Savior's coming this was practiced by such men as Anaxagoras, Democritus, and Crates, who wanted leisure time, or time for acquiring knowledge and study of dead wisdom, or empty fame and vain glory.

12. Why then is Jesus's command new or divine and life-giving, whereas the actions of people long ago brought no such benefit? If the new creation, the Son of God, offers something new, what is it? His command focuses not on the visible act, as earlier teachings had done, but on something greater, more divine, and perfect. The soul and mind are stripped of desires, and preoccupations are rooted out and discarded. This is a concept unique to the Christian and comes from the Savior himself. In former times some people viewed possessions with contempt and rejected or discarded them, but they allowed their inward passions and drives to become even stronger. They became arrogant, pretentious, conceited, and contemptuous of

other people, as though they themselves were superhuman. How could the Savior have recommended things that would be harmful and injurious to those whom he had promised eternal life? In addition, it is possible that one who has given away his possessions will then lament over what has been done and spend much time wishing the decision could be reversed. The wealth has been abandoned, but the realization that it is gone and the longing that it might be returned will become the double irritation of insecurity and regret. When someone lacks the basic necessities of life, the human spirit is broken and the desire for higher things is replaced by the constant searching to satisfy day-by-day needs.

13. How much more productive is the opposite situation, when a person possesses all that is necessary and needs to be concerned not with personal survival but with the needs of those less fortunate! How could there be any sharing if no one possessed anything? Would not such an understanding of possessions contradict and be at odds with other excellent teachings of the Lord? "Make friends for yourselves by using the mammon of unrighteousness, so that you will be received into an eternal home when it is all gone" [Luke 16:9]. "Store up treasure in heaven, where neither moth nor rust will destroy it and where thieves cannot steal it" [Matt 6:20]. How can we escape the Lord's condemnation to fire and outer darkness for not feeding the hungry, giving drink to the thirsty, clothing the naked, sheltering the homeless [Matt 25:41–43], if we ourselves do not possess these things? When the Lord was entertained by Zacchaeus, Levi, and Matthew, who were wealthy tax collectors, he did not order them to give up their possessions. Instead, he commanded that their wealth be used justly and not for their condemnation, and he promised, "Today salvation has come to his house" [Luke 19:9]. Their wealth, Jesus said, was to be shared in order to provide food for the hungry, drink for the thirsty, shelter for the homeless, and clothing for the naked. If we can only do such things if we first possess wealth, how could the Lord demand that we reject such riches? If we

did, we would not be able to share, feed, and lend support! This would make no sense at all!

14. Therefore, we must not throw away the riches [*chrēmata*] that benefit not only ourselves but our neighbors as well. They are possessions [*ktēmata*] because they are possessed [*ktēta*], and they are goods [*chrēmata*] because they are good [*chrēsima*: "useful"] and provided by God for the welfare [*chrēsin*: "use"] of all people.[4] They are under our control, and we are to use them well just as others use materials and instruments of their trade. An instrument, used with skill, produces a work of art, but it is not the instrument's fault if it is used wrongly. Wealth is such an instrument. It can be used rightly to produce righteousness. If it is used wrongly, it is the fault not of the wealth itself but of the user. Wealth is the tool, not the craftsman. We must not blame something that is neutral, being neither good nor evil in itself, but must assign responsibility to the one who chooses to use such an item either with care or negligence. As humans, we have the ability to decide how we are going to use what has been given to us. Do not regret your possessions, but destroy the passions of your soul that hinder you from using your wealth wisely. Then you may become virtuous and good and use your possessions in the most beneficial ways. The renunciation of wealth and selling of one's possessions is to be understood as the renunciation and elimination of the soul's passions. . . .

19. The truly and rightly rich person is one who is rich in virtues and capable of making a holy and faithful use of any fortune; but the falsely rich person is one who is rich according to the flesh and lives for outward possession, which is transitory and perishing, belonging now to one, now to another, and in the end to nobody at all. Again, in the same way there is a genuinely poor person and also a counterfeit and falsely named: the former is the one poor in spirit with inner personal poverty, and the latter, the one poor in a worldly sense with outward poverty. To the one poor in worldly goods but rich in vices, who is not poor in spirit and not rich toward God, God

4. Note Clement's play on words.

says: "Detach yourself from the alien possessions that are in your soul, so that you may become pure in heart and see God" [cf. Matt 5:8], which is another way of saying, "Enter into the kingdom of heaven." And how can you detach yourself from them? By selling them . . . by introducing, instead of what was formerly inherent in your soul which you desire to save, another kind of riches which provides eternal life—inward dispositions in accordance with God's command In return for these you will have endless reward and honor, and salvation, and everlasting immortality. In this way you rightly sell your surplus possessions that shut heaven against you by exchanging them for those that are able to save. Let the former be possessed by the fleshly poor, who are destitute of the latter. But you will have now treasure in heaven by receiving spiritual wealth instead.

20. The rich man, who had lived according to the law, did not understand the Lord's teaching figuratively. He could not comprehend how one can be both poor and rich, have wealth and not have wealth, use the world and not use the world. He walked away confused and sad. He gave up his desire for a better life because he felt it was beyond his ability to achieve. He saw a difficult task as an impossible one. It is difficult to keep ourselves from becoming enticed by and dependent upon the lifestyle that affluence offers, but it is not impossible. Even when surrounded by affluence we may distance ourselves from its effects and accept salvation. We center our minds on those things taught by God and strive for eternal life by using our possessions properly and with a sense of indifference toward them. Even the disciples were at first filled with fear and amazement. Why? Because they possessed wealth? They had already given up their only possessions, their nets, hooks, and fishing boats! Why, in fear, do they ask, "Who can be saved?" [Mark 10:26]. They had listened well and as good disciples perceived that the Lord had intended a deeper meaning behind the obscure parables. They realized that they had already fulfilled the command to give up one's possessions, but as newly recruited disciples of the Savior, they sensed that they had yet

to control and abolish their desires and passions. Because of this, they were extremely concerned for themselves, just as the rich man was for his need of possessions rather than his desire for eternal life. It was right that the disciples' fear should be expressed at this moment when both those having many outward possessions and those having many internal desires were categorized as being rich and denied entry into heaven. Salvation is reserved for those who are pure and without such passions and desires.

21. But the Lord responded, "With humans it is impossible, but not with God" [Mark 10:27]. Here we see great wisdom, for it impossible for us to rid ourselves of all desires and passions. If we make this our goal and earnestly desire and pursue it, the power of God will be added to our efforts. God lends support to willing souls but, if we lose our eagerness, the spirit of God is withdrawn. To save individuals against their will would be an act of force, but to rescue those who desire it is grace. The kingdom of heaven does not come to those who are lazy or asleep, but "the violent take it by force" [Matt 11:12]. This is the only good kind of force there is, to force God and to take life from God by force. God knows those who persevere, even violently persevere, and willingly gives in to them, for God welcomes such persistence. Blessed Peter, the chosen, preeminent, and first of the disciples, to whom the Lord had paid tribute [Matt 17:27], heard this and responded quickly, "We have left all and followed you" [Mark 10:28]. If Peter meant his own property, he was boasting, for as the tradition goes, he had at most four coins to leave. He has forgotten to count the kingdom of heaven as payment for the coins. As I have been saying, it is by ridding oneself of the old desires and diseases that inhabit the mind and soul that we follow the Master. Then we may seek his sinlessness and perfection and stand before him as we would a mirror, inspecting our soul and arranging everything as he would desire. . . .

26. "The first will be last and the last first" [Mark 10:31]. This saying, beneficial for its deeper meaning and interpretation, need not concern us at this point, for it applies to all people

who have accepted the faith and not merely to the wealthy. We will reserve it until later. I believe that it has been demonstrated conclusively that the Savior does not exclude the rich on account of their wealth and possessions. He has not set up obstacles to keep them from salvation, provided they submit to God's commandments, valuing their obligations more than worldly objects. They must fix their eyes on the Lord as a sailor watches the helmsman for his signals and commands. What harm has been done by one who builds economic security by careful planning and frugality prior to becoming a Christian? What is to be condemned if God, who gives life, places a child in a powerful family and a home full of wealth and possessions? If one is to be condemned for having been born into a wealthy family through no personal choice, that person would be wronged by God, who would offer a worldly life of comfort but deny eternal life. Why would wealth ever have been found within creation if it only causes death?

If an affluent person can control the power that wealth brings and remain modest and self-controlled, seeking God alone and placing God above all else, that person can follow the commandments as a poor individual, one who is free of and unconquered by the disease and wounds of wealth. If this is not the case, a camel will have a better chance to pass through the eye of a needle than such a rich person will have of entering the kingdom of God [cf. Mark 10:25]. The camel, passing through a straight and narrow way more quickly than the rich man, has another loftier meaning, which is a mystery taught by the Savior and which I discussed in my *Exposition of First Principles and Theology*.[5]

27. I would now like to explain the initial, obvious meaning of the illustration and suggest why it was used. It teaches the affluent that they must not neglect their salvation with the mistaken belief that they are already condemned; it also teaches them that they need not divest themselves of their wealth or treat it as a bitter enemy of life but, rather, must

---

5. In *Stromata* [*Miscellanies*] 3.13.1 and 3.21.2, Clement mentions a projected work on "First Principles," but it has been lost.

learn how to use it in order to gain life. People do not perish because of wealth, nor do people gain salvation merely because they think they should receive it. The Savior, however, offers hope for the wealthy and explains how the unexpected may happen and the hoped-for may become a reality. The Teacher, when asked which was the greatest commandment, replied, "You shall love the Lord your God with all your soul and with all your strength" [Mark 12:30; Matt. 22:37-38], and he pointed out that no commandment is greater than this. That is quite understandable, for the commandment deals with the first and the greatest: God our Father, through whom all things have been created and to whom all things that are saved shall return [cf. Rom 11:36]. We were loved first by him and have our existence from him. It would be blasphemous to consider any other thing greater or more excellent than him. We give him this small tribute out of gratitude for his great blessings because there is nothing else we can offer to a God who is perfect and who needs nothing from us. The very act of loving the Father to the limit of our strength and power brings us immortality. In proportion to our love of God we are drawn more closely into God.

28. The second commandment, in no way less important than the first, is this: "You shall love your neighbor as yourself" [Matt 22:39; Mark 12:31; Luke 10:27]. You must love God more than yourself. When it was asked, "Who is my neighbor?" [Luke 10:29], he did not follow Jewish custom and list such people as relatives, other Jews, proselytes, the circumcised, or the followers of the same law, but rather, told the story of a man going from Jerusalem to Jericho who was stabbed, robbed, and left nearly dead on the road. A priest passed by, as did a Levite. But a scorned and outcast Samaritan had pity on the man and, unlike the others, stopped to help. He provided all that the man needed: oil, bandages, a donkey to transport him, and payment to the innkeeper for his care. "Which of these," Jesus asked, "was a neighbor to the injured man?" When the answer was, "The one who showed pity," the Lord answered, "You must go

and do the same" [Luke 10:28–37]. Love should burst forth in good works!

29. In both commandments our Lord speaks of love, but he gives an order to our expression of that love: first we are to love God, and after that we are to love our neighbor. Who else can that mean than the Savior himself? Who, more than he, has shown pity to us, who nearly died because of those earthly powers, with fear, lust, hatred, desires, dishonesty, and pleasures? Jesus is the only one who can heal these wounds by completely cutting out those passions down to the root. He does not deal with the outward results, the bad fruit of the plant, as the law did, but his axe cuts to the roots of our wickedness. He has poured wine over our wounded souls, his blood that is from David's vine (the Eucharist). He brought to us the oil of compassion from the Father and he pours it upon us in great abundance. He has bandaged us for health and salvation, with love, faith, and hope. As a reward, he has provided angels and heavenly rulers and powers to be at our service. They too are freed from the meaninglessness of the world through the revelation of the glory of the children of God. We must love him as we do God, for God loves Christ Jesus as the one who does his will and keep his commandments. "Not everyone who says to me, Lord, Lord, will enter the kingdom of heaven, but only those who do the will of my Father" [Matt. 7:21]. "Why do you call me Lord, and then never do what I tell you?" [Luke 6:46]. . . . You will be blessed if you do what I say.

30. Those who love Christ are first; those who love and care for those who believe in him are second. Whatever is done for a Christian is accepted by the Lord as though it were done to himself, for the whole Christian community is his own. "Come, you are blessed by my Father, and enter the kingdom that was made ready for you before the world was made. I was hungry and you gave me food, and I was thirsty and you gave me drink, and I was a stranger and you took me in, I was naked and you clothed me, I was sick and you visited me, I was in prison and you came to me. . . . And the King, answering, will say to them, 'Truly I say to you, inasmuch as you have done it unto one of

the least of these my brothers and sisters, you have done it unto me'" [Matt 25:34–40]. . . .

31. He calls such people who believe in him children, little children, and friends, and also little ones here in reference to their future greatness above. "Do not despise," he says, "one of these little ones; for their angels always see the face of my Father in heaven" [Matt 18:10]. . . . He also says that the least in the kingdom of heaven, namely, his own disciple, is greater than John (the Baptizer), the greatest among those who are born of women [Matt 11:11]. . . . And again, "Make friends for yourselves by using the mammon of unrighteousness, so that you will be received into an eternal home when it is all gone" [Luke 16:9]. Christ declares that by nature all possessions are unrighteousness when we possess them only for our personal advantage, as though those are all ours and we do not bring them to the common stock for those in need. But he also declares that even from this unrighteousness we can perform a righteous and saving deed—to relieve one of those who have an everlasting habitation with the Father.

Note then, first, that he has not commanded you to be solicited or to wait to be pestered, but yourself to seek out those whom you may benefit and who are worthy disciples of the Savior. Wonderful also is the Apostle's saying, "God loves a cheerful giver" [2 Cor 9:7], who delights in giving and sows not sparingly, lest he reaps sparingly, but who shares his goods without complaint, dispute, or regret. That is pure beneficence. Better yet is the Lord's saying in another place, "Give to everyone who asks you" [Luke 6:30]; truly such is God's delight in giving. Still more divine than all is this saying—not to wait to be asked, but to personally seek after whoever is worthy of help and then to secure such a great reward of our generosity—an everlasting habitation!

32. O excellent trading! O divine business! One purchases immortality for money; and, by giving the perishing things of the world, receives in exchange for them an eternal home in heaven! Sail to this market, if you are wise, O the rich! Sail round the whole world, if need be. Spare not dangers and toils,

that you may purchase here the heavenly kingdom. Why do sparkling stones and emeralds delight you so much, and a house that is fuel for fire, or a plaything of time, or the sport of the earthquake, or an occasion for a tyrant's outrage? Aspire to dwell in heaven and to reign with God. Those in need who imitate God[6] will give you this kingdom. By receiving a little here, they will make you a dweller there with them through all ages. Beg them to take it; hasten, strive, fear lest they reject you. For they are not commanded to receive, but you to give. Moreover, the Lord did not say, "Give," "provide," "do good," or "help," but "make a friend" [Luke 16:9]. But a friend is made not by a one-time gift, but by lasting relief and companionship. For faith, love, and patience is not the work of one day, but "one that endures to the end will be saved" [Matt. 10:22].

---

6. That is, those recipients of beneficence.

3

The Acts of Thomas

The Second Act: Concerning the Apostle's coming to the King Gundaphorus[1]

17. Now when the apostle (Judas Thomas) came into the cities of India with Abban the merchant, Abban went to greet the king Gundaphorus, and reported to him about the carpenter whom he had brought with him. The king was glad, and commanded him to come before him. When he came in, the king said to him: "What trade do you know?" The apostle said to him: "Carpentry and building." The king said to him: "What craftsmanship do you know in wood and in stone?" The apostle said: "In wood, ploughs, yokes, balances, pulleys, and ships, and oars and masts; and in stone, pillars, temples, and royal palaces." And the king said: "Can you build me a palace?" He answered: "Yes, I can both build and furnish it; for this reason I have come—to build and to do the work of a carpenter."

---

1. Based on the Greek text, I have updated and revised the selected texts in this chapter from *The Apocryphal New Testament*, ed. and trans. M. R. James. (Oxford: Clarendon, 1924).

18. The king took him out of the city gates and began to discuss with him on the way the building of the palace, and how the foundations should be laid, until they came to the place where he wanted the building to be. He said: "Here is where I want the building to be." The apostle said: "Yes, this place is suitable for the building." But the place was wooded and there was much water there. So the king said: "Begin to build." But he said: "I cannot begin to build now at this season." The king said: "When can you begin?" He said: "I will begin in November and finish in April." But the king was surprised and said: "Every building is built in summer, but you can build and finish a palace in this very winter?" The apostle said: "Thus it must be; there is no other possible way." And the king said: "If this is your decision, draw me a plan of how the work is be, because I will return here after some time." The apostle then took a reed and drew, measuring the place; and he set the doors toward the east to face the light and the windows toward the west to the breezes; and the bakehouse he made toward the south and the aqueduct for the supply toward the north. The king saw it and said to the apostle: "You are truly a craftsman, and it is fitting for you to serve kings." Leaving much money with him, the king departed from him.

19. At the appointed times the king sent money and supplies, and provisions for him and the rest of the workmen. But the apostle took it all and dispensed it, going about the cities and surrounding villages, distributing it and giving alms to the poor and afflicted; and he gave them relief, saying: "The king knows that he will obtain royal recompense, but the poor should be refreshed in the present."

After these things the king sent an ambassador to the apostle with this note: "Show me what you have done, or what I should send you, or what you need." The apostle sent word to him, saying: "The palace is built and only the roof remains." When he heard it, the king sent him again gold and silver, and wrote: If the palace is built, let it be roofed." The apostle said to the Lord: "I thank you, O Lord, in all things, that you died for a short time that I may live forever in you, and that you have sold me to save many through me." And he did not cease to teach and refresh the afflicted, saying: "The Lord has dispensed this to you, and he gives to each his food; for he is the nourisher of orphans and steward of the widows, and he is relief and rest to all who are afflicted."

20. When the king came to the city he asked his friends about the palace which Judas called Thomas was building for him. They told him: "He has neither built a palace nor has he done anything of what he promised to do; but he goes about the cities and countries, and whatever he has, he gives to the poor, and teaches a new God, heals the sick, drives out demons, and does many other wonderful things. And we think he is a magician. Yet his acts of compassion and the healings done by him without compensation, and moreover his simplicity and kindness and his faith, show that he is a righteous man or an apostle of the new God whom he preaches. For he continually fasts and prays, and only eats bread with salt, and his drink is water, and he wears one garment whether in fair weather or in winter; he takes nothing from anyone, and what he has, he gives to others." When the king heard that, he hit his face with his hands, shaking his head for a long time.

21. And he sent for the merchant who had brought him, and for the apostle, and said to him: "Have you built the palace?" He said: "Yes, I have." The king said: "When shall we go and see it?" He answered and said: "You cannot see it now, but when you depart this life, then you will see it." And the king was extremely angry and commanded both the merchant and Judas called Thomas to be put in bonds and cast into prison until he should find out to whom the king's money had been given, and so destroy both him and the merchant.

And the apostle went to the prison rejoicing, and said to the merchant: "Fear nothing, but only believe in the God whom I preach, and you will be set free from this world and obtain life in the world to come." The king considered by what death he should destroy them. But when he had decided to whip them alive and burn them with fire, in the same night Gad, the king's brother, fell sick, and because of his anguish and the disappointment that the king had suffered, he was greatly depressed. He sent for the king and said to him: "O king my brother, I commit to you my house and my children; for I have been grieved because of the affront that has befallen you, and look, I am dying; and if you do not take measures against the life of that magician, you will give my soul no rest in Hades." The king said to his brother: "I have considered the whole night how I should kill him and I have decided to whip him and burn him with fire, along with the merchant who brought him."

22. As they talked together, the soul of Gad, his brother, departed. The king mourned for Gad deeply because he loved him greatly, and he commanded him to be buried in royal and precious apparel. In the meanwhile, angels took the soul of Gad, the king's brother, and carried it up to heaven, showing him the places and dwellings that were there, and asked him: "In which place would you like to dwell?" When they drew near to the building of the apostle Thomas, which he had built for the king, Gad saw it and said to the angels: "I implore you, my lords, let me to dwell in one of these lower chambers." But they said to him: "You cannot dwell in this building." He said: "Why not?" They say to him: "This is the palace that the Christian has built for your brother." He said: "I entreat you, my lords, allow me to go to my brother, that I may buy this palace from him; for my brother does not know what kind it is, and he will sell it to me."

23. Then the angels let the soul of Gad go. And as they were putting on him his grave clothes, his soul came back into him. He said to those standing around him: "Call my brother to me, that I may ask of him one request." Straightway they brought the news the king, saying: "Your brother has become alive again!" The king ran forth with a great multitude and went to his brother. Coming in, he stood by his bed amazed, unable to speak to him. His brother said: "I know and am confident, my brother, that if anyone had asked of you the half of thy kingdom, you would have given it for my sake. Therefore I beg you to grant me one favor, which I ask of you: that you sell me

what I ask from you." The king answered and said: "What is it that you ask me to sell you?" He said: "Convince me by an oath that you will grant it me." And the king swore to him: "Whatever of my possessions you ask, I will give you." He said to him: "Sell me that palace which you have in the heaven." The king said: "From where should I have a palace in heaven?" He said: "The one that Christian built for you, who is now in the prison, whom the merchant brought to you, having purchased him from a certain Jesus. I mean that Hebrew slave whom you wished to punish, having suffered deception from, because of whom I was grieved and died, and am now alive again."

24. Then the king, considering the matter, understood his words about the eternal benefits which should come to him and which concerned him, and said: "That palace I cannot sell you, but I pray to enter into it and dwell there and be counted worthy to belong to its inhabitants. But if you truly wish to buy such a palace, look, the man is alive and will build you a better one than that." Immediately he sent and brought out of prison the apostle and the merchant who was shut up with him, saying: "I entreat you, as a man entreating the servant of God, to pray for me and beseech him, whose servant you are, to forgive me and overlook what I have done to you or planned to do; and that I may become a worthy inhabitant of that dwelling for which I have done nothing, but you have built it for me, laboring alone, by the grace of your God working in you; and that I also may become a servant and serve this God whom you preach." And his brother also fell down before the apostle and said: "I entreat and supplicate before your God that I may become worthy of his service, and that I may be worthy of sharing what was shown to me by his angels."

25. The apostle, filled with joy, said: "I praise you, O Lord Jesus, that you have revealed your truth in these men. For you alone are the God of truth, and no other; and you are he who knows all things that are unknown to the most; you, Lord, are he who in all things shows compassion and mercy to people. For mortals, because of the error in them, have overlooked you but you have not overlooked them. Now at my supplication and

request, receive the king and his brother and join them to your fold, cleansing them with your washing and anointing them with your oil from the error that encompasses them. Keep them also from the wolves and bring them into your meadows. Give them a drink out of your immortal fountain, which is neither fouled nor dries up. For they entreat and beseech you and wish to become your servants and ministers, and for this they are content even to be persecuted by your enemies, and for your sake to suffer hatred, mockery, and even death, as you suffered all these things for our sake in order to preserve us. You are Lord and truly the good shepherd. Grant them that they may have confidence in you alone, and obtain the help that comes from you and the hope of their salvation, which they expect from you alone; and that they may be established in your mysteries and receive the perfect good of your graces and gifts, and flourish in your ministry and come to perfection in your Father."

26. Being well disposed to the apostle, both the king Gundaphorus and his brother Gad followed him, never leaving him; they also provided for those in need, giving to all and refreshing all. And they besought him that they might also receive the seal of the word (i.e., baptism), saying to him: "Seeing that our souls are at ease and we are earnest for God, give us the seal. For we have heard you say that the God whom you preach knows his own sheep by his seal." The apostle said to them: "I also rejoice and entreat you to receive this seal, and to partake with me in this eucharist and feast of blessing of the Lord, and to be made perfect by it. For this is the Lord and God of all, Jesus Christ whom I preach, and he is the father of truth, in whom I have taught you to believe." And he commanded them to bring oil, that they might receive the seal by the oil.

The Eleventh Act: Concerning the Wife of Misdaeus[2]

136. When Tertia[3] heard this by Mygdonia,[4] she said: "I pray

2. The king of India.
3. King Misdaeus's wife.

you, sister, bring me to that stranger (the apostle Thomas) who teaches these great things, that I also may go and hear him, and be taught to worship the God whom he preaches, and join in his prayers and all of which you have told me." Mygdonia said to her: "He is in the house of Siphor the captain; for he became the occasion of life for all who are being saved in India." Upon hearing that, Tertia went quickly to Siphor's house to see the new apostle that had come to the country. When she entered, Judas said to her: "What have you come to see? A stranger, poor, contemptible, and needy, who has neither riches nor possession? Yet my one possession which neither kings nor rulers can take away, which neither perishes nor comes to an end, is Jesus the Savior of all humanity, the Son of the living God, who has given life to all who believe in him and take refuge in him; and he is known by the number of his servants." Tertia said to him: "May I partake of this life, as you promise, that all will receive who come together to the house of God?" The apostle said: "The treasury of the holy king is opened wide, and those who worthily partake of the goods stored there rest, and by resting they reign. But first, no one unclean and vile comes to him. For he knows our inmost hearts and the depths of our thought, and none can escape him. You, then, if you truly believes in him, you will be made worthy of his mysteries; and he will make you great and rich, and an heir of his Kingdom."

The Thirteenth Act: Vazan Receives Baptism with Others

156. Judas began to pray and say: "O companion and defender, and hope of the weak and confidence of the poor; refuge and shelter of the wear; voice which came forth from on high; comforter who dwells in our midst; port and harbor of those who pass through the regions of darkness; physician who heals

---

4. The wife of Charisius, the relative of the king Misdaeus. She had been introduced by the apostle Thomas to the ascetic Christian gospel, which drew a sharp contrast between earthly and heavenly marriage and also earthly and heavenly riches. Upon her conversion, she became an ascetic follower of Thomas, renouncing her marital relationship with her husband, Charisius, and her temporal possessions.

without payment, who was crucified among people for many, who descended into hell with great might, whose sight the princes of death could not endure; and you ascended with great glory; . . . Son of mercy, the Son who was sent to us out of love for humanity from the perfect fatherland above, the Lord of undefiled possessions; who serves your servants that they may live; who fills the creation with your riches; the poor one, who was in need and hungry forty days; who satisfies thirsty souls with your goods; be with Vazan, Misdaeus' son, and Tertia and Mnesara, and gather them into your fold and gather into your fold. . . ."

The Martyrdom of the Apostle Thomas

145. "My mouth is not sufficient to praise you, neither am I able to conceive the care and providence which have had for me. For I desired to gain riches, but you by a vision showed me that they are full of loss and injury to those who gain them; and I believed your revelation, and continued in the poverty of the world until you, the true riches, were revealed to me, who filled both me and the rest who were worthy of you with your own riches and set free your own from care and anxiety. I have therefore fulfilled your commandments, O Lord, and accomplished your will, and become poor and needy and a stranger and a slave and despised and a prisoner and hungry and thirsty and naked and barefoot; and I have toiled for your sake, that my confidence might not perish, my hope in you might not be confounded, my hard labor might not be in vain, and my weariness might be counted for nothing. . . .

146. "The money which you have given me I laid down upon the table of the money-changers; when you require it, restore this to me with usury, as you have promised. With your one mina I have traded and have made ten; you have added more to me beside what I had, as you covenanted. I have forgiven my debtor the mina—do not require it at my hands. I was called to the dinner, and I came; and I refused the land, the yoke of oxen, and the wife, that I might not be rejected for their sake;

I was called to the wedding, and I put on white raiment, that I might be worthy of it and not be bound hand and foot and cast into the outer darkness. My lamp with its bright light expects the master coming from the marriage, that it may receive him, and I may not see it dimmed because the oil is spent. My eyes, O Christ, look upon you, and my heart exults with joy because I have fulfilled your will and perfected your commandments; that I may be likened to that watchful and careful servant who in his eagerness does not neglect to keep vigil. All the night have I labored to keep my house from robbers, lest it be broken through. . . .

147. "The plough-land has become white and the harvest has come, that I may receive my wages. My garment that grows old I have worn out, and the labor that has brought me to rest I have accomplished. I have kept the first watch and the second and the third, that I may behold your face and adore your holy brightness. I have pulled down the barns and left them desolate upon earth, that I may be filled full from your treasures. . . . I have received reproach upon earth, but give me the return and the recompense in the heavens."

4

Tertullian

Against Marcion[1]

4.15 [On Luke 6:24: "Woe to you who are rich, for you have already received your comfort"] . . . Again, since the "woe" which has the rich in view is the Creator's, it is not Christ, but the Creator, who is angry with the rich; and Christ approves of the rich's claims—I mean, their pride and glory, their devotion to the world and neglect of God, for which they deserve that "woe" from the Creator. And surely this disapproval of the rich must proceed from the same [Christ] who has just now expressed approval of the indigent [Luke 6:20]. There is nobody but reprobates the opposite of what he has approved. Thus, if that curse against the rich is ascribed to the Creator, the blessing of the poor must also be claimed for him, and in that case the whole work of Christ is the work of the Creator. If the blessings meant for the poor is to be ascribed to Marcion's god, the cursing meant for the rich must also be set down to him; and in

---

1. Translation of Tertullian's texts is mine.

that case he will be exactly like the Creator, a kind god and also a judge, and there will no longer be room for that distinction by which there comes to be two gods; and when this distinction is removed, there will remain the truth which pronounces the Creator to be the only God there is. Therefore, if "woe" is a term of malediction, or of some unusually severe reproof, and if it is by Christ uttered against the rich, I have to show that the Creator also disapproves of the rich, as I have already shown that he is a comforter of the poor, so that I may prove Christ to be on the Creator's side in this matter. If the Creator made Solomon rich [1 Kgs 3:5–13], this was because when given the choice, Solomon preferred asking for what he knew to be well-pleasing to God—wisdom and understanding—and thus was worthy to obtain the riches, which he did not prefer. And yet, granting one indeed riches is not out of character with God; for both the rich are comforted and assisted by these; and many works of justice and charity are performed with them.

But there are serious faults accompanying riches; and it is because of these that "woes" are declared to the rich in the Gospel: "For you have already received your comforted"; that is, from your riches, because of the reputation and the worldly benefits they bring. And so in Deuteronomy, Moses says: "Lest when you have eaten and are full, and have built great houses, and your sheep and you oxen are multiplied, and your silver and gold, your heart be lifted up and you forget the Lord your God" [Deut 8:12–14]. So also against the king Hezekiah when he became proud of this treasures and boasted of them rather than of God. . . . So also he [Creator] attacked the daughters of Zion by Isaiah when they were haughty through luxury and abundance of riches [Isa 3:16–24], just as in another passage he utters threats against the high-born and the proud: "Hell has enlarged his soul and opened his mouth, and the nobles, and the great, and the rich"—here will be Christ's "woe to the rich"—"shall go down there, and a man shall be brought low"—evidently one exalted by riches—"and a mighty man shall be dishonored"—obviously one honored for his possession's sake [Isa 5:14]. And concerning these again: "Behold, the

Lord of hosts shall shatter the boughs with strength, and the high ones shall be smitten down, and the haughty shall fall by the sword" [Isa 10:33]. And who are these but the rich?

I have done no more than to show that the Creator dissuading people from riches, and not also condemning the rich in advance, and that with the very same words that Christ also used. However, no one could deny that the threat added against the rich by that "woe" of Christ, came from the same authority from whom also had first proceeded the dissuasion against the material sin of these persons, that is, their riches. For a threat is something added to dissuasion. He utters a "woe" also to "the full because they will go hungry; also to those who laugh now, for they shall mourn" [Luke 6:25].

4.36 [On Luke 18] . . . When a certain man asked him [Jesus], "Good Teacher, what shall I do to obtain possession of eternal life?" [18:18], Jesus inquired whether he knew—which means, whether he kept—the commandments of the Creator, so as to testify that it was by the Creator's commandments that eternal life is acquired. Then, when the man replied that from his youth up he had kept all the principal commandments, Jesus said to him: "One thing you lack; sell all that you have and give to the poor, and you shall have treasure in heaven; and come, follow me" [18:21–22]. Well now, Marcion, and all you companions in misery and associates in the offensiveness of that heretic, what will you dare say to this? Did Christ here rescind those former commandments: "Do not kill, do not commit adultery, do not steal, do not bear false witness, honor your father and mother?" Or did he both keep them and add what was lacking? (This commandment of distributing to the poor, however, is spread out everywhere in the law and the prophets [i.e., the Old Testament].)This boastful keeper of the commandments was therefore convicted of holding money in much higher esteem. So then this truth of the Gospel stands valid: "I have not come to destroy the law and the prophets, but rather to fulfill them" [Matt 5:17]. At the same time, he also dissipated doubts about other questions, when he declared that the name of God and of the supremely Good belonged to the one and the same being, and that eternal life and treasure in heaven, and himself, too, pertain to that One—whose commandments he both maintained and enriched with his own supplementary precepts. So he is to be recognized as in agreement with the following passage in Micah, which says: "He has shown you, O mortal, what is good; and what does the Lord requires of you, but to do justice, to love mercy, and to be ready to follow the Lord your God?" [Mic 6:8] Now Christ is that man who tells us that is good: the knowledge of the law. He says, "You know the commandments": to do justice; "Sell all that you have": to love mercy; "And give to the poor": to be ready to walk with the Lord; "And come, follow me," says he.

♂ Listen to his commands

On Patience

7. The entire practice of patience is compressed within this fundamental precept whereby not even a lawful injury is permitted. But now, while we run through the causes of impatience, all the other precepts, too, will correspond in their own context. If you are disturbed by the loss of property, then, in practically every passage of the holy Scriptures one is admonished to despise the world. And one can find no greater exhortation to an indifference toward money than the example of our Lord himself who did not own any worldly riches. He always justifies the poor and condemns the rich. Thus he has set disdain for wealth ahead of the endurance of losses, pointing out through his rejection of riches that one should make no account of the loss of them. Hence, we need not seek wealth, since our Lord did not seek it; and we ought to bear the deprivation or even the theft of it without regret. The Spirit of the Lord, through the Apostle, has called the desire of money [*cupiditas*] the root of all evils [1 Tim 6:10].

We should interpret that this desire of money does not consist only in the desire for another person's property. Even what seems to be our own belongs to another; for nothing is our own, since all things belong to God to whom we, too, belong. Therefore, if we feel impatient when we suffer some loss, we exhibit that we entertain a desire for money, since we grieve over the loss of what is not our own. We are seeking what belongs to another when we are unwilling to bear the loss of what belongs to another. The one who is upset and unable to bear one's loss sins, you might say, against God himself by preferring the things of earth to those of heaven. For, the soul which one has received from the Lord is upset by the attractiveness of worldly goods. *Don't be upset for losses*

Let us then, with willing hearts, relinquish earthly goods that we may preserve those of heaven! Let the whole world fall in ruins provided I gain the patience to endure it! In truth, people who have not resolved to bear with fortitude a slight loss *loss of goods* occasioned by theft, violence, or even by their own stupidity, will not readily or willingly touch what they own for the sake *argue* of charity. For who that refuses to undergo any operation at all at the hands of another, puts a knife to one's own body? Patience to endure, shown on occasions of loss, is a training in giving and sharing. Those who do not fear loss are not reluc- *Key* tant to give. Otherwise, how would one who has two tunics give one of them [Luke 3:11] to the destitute, unless the same is one who can offer his cloak as well to the one going off with his tunic [Matt 5:40]? How will we make friends for ourselves with mammon [Luke 16:9] if we love it only to the extent that we do not share in its loss? We shall perish together with the lost mammon. What do we find here, where it is our business to lose?

It is for pagans to be unable to sustain all loss; they would set worldly goods before their life perhaps. And they do this when, in their eager desire for wealth, they engage in lucrative but dangerous commerce on the sea; when for money's sake, they unhesitatingly engage in transactions also in the forum, even though there be reason to fear loss; they do it, in fine, when they hire themselves out for the games and military service, or when, in desolate regions, they commit robbery regardless of the wild beasts. On the contrary, since we are different from them, it befits us to give up not our life for money but money for our life, either by voluntary charity or by the patient endurance of loss.

5

Cyprian of Carthage

On the Lapsed[1]

11. My beloved, we must not conceal the truth; we must not keep silent about the true nature and cause of our wound. Blind love of one's patrimony has deceived many; they could have not been prepared or ready for departing when their possessions bound them like fetters. Those fetters are for those who remained, those chains by which virtue was shacked, and faith hard pressed, and mind bound, and the soul imprisoned, so that they who clung to earthly things became as booty and food for the serpent who, according to God's sentence, feeds upon earth. Therefore the Lord, the teacher of good things, warning for the future, says: "If you will be perfect, sell all your possessions and give to the poor and you shall have treasure in heaven; and come, follow me" [Matt 19:21; cf. Mark 10:21; Luke 18:22]. If the rich did this, they would not perish by their riches; if they laid up treasure in heaven, they would

---

1. My translation.

not now have an enemy and assailant in their own household; their heart and mind and feeling would be in heaven, if their treasure were in heaven; no one could be overcome by the world, who had nothing in the world with which to be overcome. They would follow the Lord, loosed and free, as the apostles and many in apostolic times, and as some others often did since, leaving their possessions and their parents, clung to the undivided ties of Christ.

12. But how can they follow Christ, who are held back by the chain of their patrimony? Or, how can they seek heaven, and climb to the sublime and lofty heights, who are weighed down by earthly desires? They think that they possess when they are rather possessed; they are slaves of their own property, not masters as regards their money but its bond-slaves. The Apostle refers to this time, to these very people, when he says: "But those who seek to become rich fall into temptation and a snare and into many harmful desires which plunge people into destruction and damnation. For the desire of money is the root of all evils, and some coveting riches have strayed from the faith and have involved themselves in many sorrows" [1 Tim 6:9–10]. But with what rewards does the Lord invite us to have contempt for personal wealth? What compensations does he make for these small and trifling losses of this present time? "There is no one," he says, "who has left house, or land, or parents, or brothers, or wife, or children for the kingdom of God's sake, who shall not receive a seven-fold in this present time, and in the world to come life everlasting" [Luke 18:29–30]. If we know these things and have found them out from the truth of God who makes the promise, not only should we not fear such losses but we should even desire them, for the Lord himself again proclaims and gives warning: "Blessed shall you be when they persecute you, and separate you and cast you out and reject your name as evil because of the Son of man. Rejoice on that day and leap for joy, for behold your reward is great in heaven" [Luke 6:22–23].

35. But you, beloved, who are responsive to the fear of the Lord and whose minds, despite your fall, are mindful of their

evils, look into your sins in repentance and grief; recognize the very serious crime of your conscience, open the eyes of your hearts to an understanding of your shortcomings, neither despairing of the mercy of the Lord nor yet claiming immediate pardon. As God in his fatherly affection is always forgiving and good, so in his majesty as Judge he is to be feared. Let us weep as greatly, corresponding to the extent of our sin. For such a deep wound there should no lack of a careful and prolonged treatment; let the repentance be no less than the crime. Do you think that God can be easily appeased, whom you denied with treacherous words, above whom you set your property, and whose temple you polluted with sacrilegious contamination? Do you think that he will easily have mercy on you, whom you have declared not to be your God? You must pray and entreat more intently, to spend the day grieving, to spend your nights in vigils and tears, to spend all your time in mournful lamentation; to cling to ashes lying stretched on the ground; to wallow in sackcloth and filth; to wish for no garment now after losing the cloak of Christ; to prefer fasting after the devil's food; to devote yourself to righteous works by which sins are purged; to apply yourself frequently to almsgiving, by which souls are freed from death [cf. Tob 12:8]. What the adversary tried to take away, let Christ receive; your property must not be retained now or loved, by which you have been both deceived and conquered. Such wealth is to be avoided as an enemy, to be fled as a thief, to be feared by its possessors as a sword and poison. What has remained should be of benefit, only to this end that the crime and sin may be redeemed by it. Let your good works [i.e., almsgiving] be done without delay and in abundance; let all your wealth be expended on the healing of the wound; let us lend our goods and means to the Lord, who is to be our Judge [cf. Prov 19:17]. Thus faith flourished under the apostles' time; thus the first people of the believers kept Christ's commands—they were prompt; they were generous; they gave all to be distributed by the apostles, and yet they had no such sins to redeem [cf. Acts 2:44–45, 4:32–34].

36. If people perform prayer with their whole heart, if they

mourn with genuine lamentations and tears of repentance, if they turn the Lord to forgive their sin by continual righteous works, such people can receive his mercy, who has offered his mercy with these words: "When you turn and lament, then you shall be saved and shall know where you have been" and again: "I have no pleasure in the death of the dying, says the Lord, but that they should return and live" [Ezek 18:32; cf. 18:23, 33:11]. And the prophet Joel declares the Lord's mercy in the Lord's own words: "Turn," he says, "to the Lord your God, for he is gracious and merciful, patient and abounding in mercy and relents his thought from the evil that has been done" [Joel 2:13]. He can grant mercy; he can turn back his judgment. He can mercifully pardon those who are repentant, who perform good works, who beseech. He can regard as acceptable whatever the martyrs have sought and the priests have done on their behalf. Or, if anyone moves him more by his own atonements, if one appeases his wrath, his rightful indignation by righteous supplication, he arms again those who have suffered defeat. He restores and invigorates their strength so that their restored faith may flourish. The soldiers will seek their contest again; they will repeat their fight; they will provoke the enemy; through suffering they have indeed become stronger for the battle. Those who have made such satisfaction to God, by repentance for their deeds and by shame for their sins, have conceived more of both virtue and faith from the very sorrow for their fall. They, after being heard and aided by the Lord, will cause the church to rejoice, which they had recently saddened, and will merit not only God's forgiveness, but a crown.

On Works and Almsgiving[2]

1. Many and great are the gifts that have been and still are given to us by God the Father and Christ, who has worked and is always working for our salvation! The Father sent his Son to

---

2. Translation of this text, except par. 23, comes from Jan L. Womer, ed. and trans., *Morality and Ethics in Early Christianity* (Sources of Early Christian Thought; Philadelphia: Fortress, 1987).

rescue us and to give us life so that we might be restored to him. The Son was willing to be sent as the Son of man so that he could make us children of God. He humbled himself so that a devastated race might be raised to life again; he was wounded so that he could heal our wounds; he became a slave in order to free those in bondage; he accepted death so that he could give immortality to mortals. These are the many and great examples of divine compassion! But, in addition to this, his great compassion and love also provides the means by which we are given further support even after we have been redeemed. When the Lord came to earth, he healed the wounds that Adam had given to humanity and he provided an antidote to the poisons of the old serpent. He gave a law to those who had been made whole and commanded that they should sin no more, for fear of worse things that might happen to the sinner. We were limited and confined by the restrictions of our naiveté. Our weak human strength had to be supplemented with the divine mercy that was given once again to guide us toward salvation. We have been given works of justice and mercy to do, so that our almsgiving will wash away the pollutions we later contract in our lives.

2. The Holy Spirit speaks in the divine Scriptures and says, "By almsgiving and faith sins are purged" [cf. Prov 16:6]. Those are not the sins that we committed earlier, for they were forgiven by Christ's blood and sanctification. It also says, "As water extinguishes a fire, so almsgiving atones for sin" [Sir 3:30]. Here it also shows that, just as the supply of saving water quenches the fire of Gehenna, so also the flame of sin is smothered by almsgiving and works of justice. Because in baptism the remission of sins is granted once and for all, so in works of charity that flow from the baptized person, the mercy of God continues to be manifested. The Lord teaches this in the Gospel when he responds to a criticism that the disciples eat before washing their hands: "He who made the outside also made the inside; gave alms and everything is clean for you" [Luke 11:40–41]. This has taught us that not the hands but the heart should be washed so that the filth within is removed, and

not merely that which is on the outside. Those who are clean on the inside will be clean on the outside as well. If we cleanse our mind, the cleansing of our skin and body will also begin.

Furthermore, he admonishes us and points out the way in which we may become clean and purified: by the giving of alms. He who teaches and warns us in mercy asks us to show mercy, and he who seeks salvation for those whom he already redeemed at a great price, teaches that they may be washed a second time if they have soiled themselves after receiving the grace of baptism.

3. Let us acknowledge, dear friends, this saving gift of divine mercy. Since none of us can be free of some wounds to our conscience, let us receive the healing that washes away our sins. None of us should flatter ourselves with the belief that we have a pure and spotless heart or that we are innocent and without need of medicine for our wounds. It is written, "Who can say that they have a pure heart or that they are free from sin?" [Prov 20:9]. John says, "If we say that we have no sin, we deceive ourselves, and the truth is not in us" [1 John 1:8]. If no one can be without sin, even those who are proud or foolish and do not admit it, we can see how necessary and compassionate the divine mercy is toward us. God knows that those who were healed in baptism will suffer more wounds in life, and he has provided additional remedies to save them.

4. Most beloved, the divine instruction of both the Old and New Testaments has never compromised or failed in admonishing God's people to works of mercy. The Holy Spirit calls and exhorts each of us to hope for eternal life and to give alms. God commanded Isaiah, "Cry aloud, do not give up. Life up your voice like a trumpet and declare to my people their transgressions, and to the house of Jacob their sins" [Isa 58:1]. God commanded that their sins be condemned and the divine wrath be made known. Pleading, prayers, and fasting were not sufficient ways to make amends; sackcloth and ashes were not accepted as a way to soften God's anger. The only way to appease God is through almsgiving and works of mercy. "Share your bread with the hungry and bring the poor and the homeless into your

house. When you see the naked, give them clothing and do not reject your own children. Then your light will break forth as the dawn; you will quickly gain good health; your righteousness will be seen by all and the glory of God will surround you. Then when you cry out, God will answer you, and while you are still asking, he will reply, 'Here I am'" [Isa 58:7–9].

5. The remedies in which we may appease God are described for us by God himself: the Scriptures have taught what sinners should do. God is satisfied when we do works of justice, and sins are forgiven through acts of mercy. In Solomon we read, "Store up your alms in the hearts of the poor and they will intercede for you against any evil" [Sir 29:12], and, "Whoever refuses to hear the cry of the poor will cry to God and not be heard" [Prov 21:13]. Those who have not shown mercy will not be given mercy by the Lord; those who have not responded to the prayer of the poor will not receive a divine response to their own prayer. In the Psalms the Holy Spirit declares and affirms, "Blessed are those who consider the poor, for the Lord will deliver them when they face trouble" [Ps 41:1]. Daniel remembered this when King Nebuchadnezzar was in trouble after his frightening dream. In order to seek God's help in averting disaster, he advised the king, "Therefore, O King, listen to my advice; seek forgiveness for your sins by practicing righteousness, and for your gross injustice by showing justice to the oppressed. Then God will give you peace" [Dan 4:27]. Because the king did not follow this advice, he endured the misfortunes and disasters that he had seen in his dream. He could have avoided and escaped this fate if he had redeemed his sins by giving alms. The angel Raphael teaches the same thing and commands that alms be given freely and in great quantity: "Prayer is good when combined with fasting and almsgiving. Almsgiving preserves one from death and wipes away all sin" [Tob 12:8–10]. This shows that our prayer and fasting bring better results when combined with almsgiving, and that our requests to God are granted more fully when they are accompanied by works of mercy and justice. The angel reveals and assures us that our prayers become more effica-

cious through our almsgiving and that such acts of mercy protect us from dangers and rescue our souls from death. . . .

23. How do we reply to the arguments and excuses of the rich who refuse to give alms? How can we defend the wealthy whose minds are barren and confused? How can we excuse them when we are even lower than the devil's servants and are not willing to repay Christ for the price of his passion and death even in small ways? He has given us commands and taught us what we should do. He has promised rewards to those who give and share freely, and he has threatened the unfruitful with punishment. He has made it clear how he will judge humanity and what his final sentence will be. What excuse is left for the lazy? What defense for those whose lives bear no good fruit? If the servant does not do what he is told, he will receive the punishment that was threatened. "When the Son of man comes in glory, and all the angels with him, then he will sit on the throne in glory and the nations will be gathered before him. He will separate them as a shepherd divides the sheep from the goats, and he will place the sheep on his right side and the goats on his left. Then the King will say to those on his right, 'Come. O blessed of my Father, inherit the kingdom prepared for you from the foundation of the world, for I was hungry and you gave me food; I was thirsty and you gave me water; I was a stranger and you accepted me into your home; naked and you gave me clothing; sick and you visited me; in prison and you came to me.' Then the righteous will ask him, 'Lord, when did we see you hungry, thirsty, or naked? When did we see you sick or in prison and come to you?' The King will answer, 'Truly, I say to you, when you did it for one of the least of my children, you did it to me.' [The text from Matt 25:31–46 continues, concluding: Those who fail to do these things] will go away to eternal punishment, but the righteous will enter eternal life."

What greater things could Christ say to us? What better way could he encourage us to works of justice and mercy than to say that such acts are done to himself and that he is offended when we fail to reach out to the poor and needy? Those in the church who are not moved to help a brother or sister may be encouraged when they see how Christ is involved, and those who do not help the suffering may remember that our Lord is in that person who needs our help.

24. Therefore, dearly beloved, you live with deep reverence for God, and you have rejected the things of the world in order to set your thoughts on things heavenly and divine. Let us offer our complete faith, our devout minds, our obedience, and our continual labors to the Lord that he may be pleased with us. Let us give earthly garments to Christ so that we receive heavenly robes; let us share food and drink in this world so that we may join Abraham, Isaac, and Jacob at the heavenly banquet. So that we do not receive a minimal harvest, let us sow in great quantity. While there is time, let us seek security and eternal salvation. The Apostle Paul says, "While we have the opportunity, let us do good to all people, and especially to those who are of the household of faith. Let us not grow weary of doing good, for in time we shall reap the rewards" [Gal 6:9–10].

25. We need to remember what the lives of the first believers were like at the time of the apostles. They were filled with great virtues and burned with the warmth of their new faith. They sold their houses and farms and gladly gave all they had to the apostles for distribution to the poor [cf. Acts 4:34–35]. By freeing themselves and selling their earthly possessions, they transferred their title to the eternal land and its fruits, homes that would be theirs for eternity. This was the reward for their many good works and their unity in love. In the Acts of the Apostles we read, "Now the company of believers acted with one heart and soul, for there was no distinction among them and no one claimed possession of anything, for all was owned in common" [Acts 4:32]. Surely this is the way to become children of God by spiritual birth; this is the way to follow the heavenly law and to imitate the equity of God the Father. Whatever God has is given to us to use, and no person is denied the opportunity to receive God's blessings and gifts. The light of day, the radiance of the sun, the rain, and the wind are given to all. Everyone shares the same sleep and the beauty of the

moon and stars. In the same spirit of equality we on earth share our possessions freely and justly with the community in imitation of God the Father.

26. What then, my dearly beloved, will be the reward for those who practice charity? The Lord will gather his people and distribute the rewards he has promised in accordance with their good works and merits. With great and overflowing joy they will receive heavenly things for earthly ones, eternal for temporal, and great for small. Our Lord will offer us to the Father as those whom he has restored by his sanctification. Through the shedding of his blood we will be raised to eternity and immortality, and paradise will be opened to us. We will enter heaven itself in the faith of his true promises! Think over these things and accept them completely in faith, love them with your whole heart, and let them become alive in your life of continual works of mercy. Those saving works of mercy are a glorious and divine thing, a great comfort to believers, a salutary safeguard of our security, a defense for our hope, a guarding of our faith, a cure for sin. Such actions are within your power to perform, and they are at the same time great but easy. They offer you a crown of peace without the risk of persecution. They are true and great service of God; they are necessary for the weak, glorious to the strong, a way for the Christian to receive spiritual grace, a positive recommendation for us before Christ the Judge, and a way of making God our debtor [cf. Prov 19:17]. Let us work willingly and immediately to receive this badge of salvation. In this contest of righteousness, let us run with Christ and God watching us, and let us not slacken our pace with desires for this life and this world, for we have now begun a race that is greater than what this world and this office can offer. If the day of reward or of persecution should come, the Lord will not fail to reward the merits of those who have persevered in the contest of doing justice and mercy. In time of peace he gives conquerors the white crown for their labors; in time of persecution we receive a purple crown as a reward for giving our life.

6

Lactantius

The Divine Institutes[1]

5.14. . . . The two veins of justice are piety and equality (*aequitas*); all justice springs from these fountains. While piety forms its source and origin, equity provides all its energy and method.

Piety is none other than the knowledge of God, as appropriately defined by Trismegistus elsewhere. If indeed piety is to know God, and the heart of this knowledge is to worship him, anyone who does not know God does not know justice. For how can you know justice for itself when you do know its source?

The other part of justice is equality; by equality I do not mean the virtue of good judgment, which is itself praiseworthy in a just person, but making oneself equal to everyone else, what Cicero calls "equality of status" [*Rep.* 1.27.43]. God who created human beings and gave them the breath of life wanted

---

1. Based on the Latin text, I have revised and expanded Peter C. Phan's translation in *Social Thought* (Message of the Fathers of the Church 20; Wilmington, DE: Glazier, 1984). Used by permission.

all to be equal. He instituted all the same conditions of living for everyone; he made us all capable of wisdom; he promised immortality to all; no one is cut off from God's heavenly benefits. Just as God distributes his light equally to all, sends forth his fountains to all, supplies food, and gives the sweet rest of sleep to all, so he bestows equity and virtue on all. With him no one is a slave and no one is a master; for if he is the same father to all, we are all his children with equal rights. No one is poor in God's eyes except the one lacking justice; no one is rich except the one full of virtues; moreover, no one is excellent except the one with goodness and innocence; no one is most renowned except the one with abundant works of mercy; no one is more perfect except the one having fulfilled virtue in all degrees. Therefore, neither the Romans nor the Greeks could possess justice because they kept people distinct in different levels from the poor to the rich, from the humble to the powerful, from common people to the highest authorities of kings. Where people are not all equal, there is no equality; and inequality excludes justice of itself. The whole force of justice lies in the fact that it makes equal everyone who comes into this human condition on equal terms. . . .

6.12. This is that perfect justice which sustains human society, of which philosophers speak. This is the greatest and truest fruit of riches: not to use wealth for one's own personal pleasure, but for the welfare of many; and not for one's own immediate enjoyment, but for justice, which alone endures. We must therefore keep in mind, that the hope of receiving in return must certainly be absent from the exercise of mercy. Rather, we should expect the reward of this work from God alone; for if you look for it in people, then it will not be humanity [humanitas], but lending of a benefit at interest; you cannot earn any credit when you do what you do, not for another person but for yourself. And yet there is a return: whatever people do for another, expecting nothing in return, they really do for themselves, for they will receive a reward from God. God also enjoins that if we ever prepare a banquet, we should invite those who cannot invite and repay us in return, so that every act of our life is its exercise of mercy [cf. Luke 14:13–14]. However, we should not think that we are forbidden from entertaining our friends or showing kindness to our neighbors. God has revealed to us what our true and just work is: we must live with our neighbors, based on knowing that the one manner of living relates to humans, the other to God.

Therefore, hospitality is a prime virtue, as the philosophers also say; but they separate it from true justice and force it under personal expediency. Cicero says: "Theophrastus rightly praises hospitality. It is highly attractive, as it also appears to me, that the homes of illustrious men to be open to illustrious guests." But he is wrong, in the same way that he was wrong when he commended bestowing "bounty on suitable people." The house of a just and wise man ought to be open not to the illustrious but to the poor and miserable. Those illustrious and powerful men cannot be in need of anything, since they are sufficiently protected and honored by their own wealth. . . . The principle of justice is at work only in those good deeds . . . [that] are done to people who can in no way profit us. In entertaining distinguished men, Cicero looked only to his own advantage. . . . For he says, "Anyone doing that will become powerful abroad by the favor of the important people, whose interest he has safeguarded by hospitality and friendship." . . .

The ransoming of captives is a great and noble work of justice, of which the same Cicero also approved. . . . It is a proper work for the just to care for the poor and to ransom prisoners, since the people who do this are called the great and eminent by the unjust; it is a matter of a great praise because they made such benefactions to the people who were not expected to receive. . . . Justice therefore exists where there is no obligation of necessity for doing good. . . .

Nor is it less a great work of justice to protect and defend children and widows who are destitute and in need of help. This is the divine law prescribed for all, since all the good judges regard it part of their duty to favor them with natural humanity and to strive to help them. . . .

Also, caring for and cherishing the sick who have no one to

assist them is a work of the greatest humanity and beneficence. Whoever does this brings a living sacrifice to God, and what he gives to another in time, he will receive from God in eternity.

The last and greatest duty of piety is the burial of strangers and the poor, something which those teachers of virtue and justice have not even mentioned. They measured all duties by the advantage to them and so could not see it. . . . We, however, are not discussing what is bearable for a wise man but what his duty is. Thus, we are not asking whether the whole matter of burial is useful or not; but even if it is useless, as they think, still it must be done for this reason alone, that it seems to be a good and humane thing to do among people. The feeling is questioned and the purpose is weighed. Therefore, we will not allow the image and workmanship of God to fall prey to wild beasts and birds, but we will return it to the earth, from where it came. . . .

The whole nature of justice lies in our providing for others through humanity what we provide for our own families and relatives through affection. This kindness is much more sure and just when it is offered, not to people who are imperceptible, but to God alone, to whom a just work is a most acceptable sacrifice. Perhaps someone will say: "If I will do all these things, I will have no possessions. If a great number of people falls in poverty, gets sick, is taken captive, or die, that anyone doing such acts must be stripped of his property even in a day, am I to throw away the family fortune, whether it is acquired by my own labor or by that of my ancestors, so that I myself have to live on the mercy of others?"[2]

Why do you so faint-heartedly fear poverty? Even your philosophers approve of it, affirming that there is nothing safer or more peaceful! What you are fearful is the haven of anxieties. Do you not know how many dangers and how many accidents you are exposed to with all this evil wealth? It will treat you well if it all goes without shedding your blood. But

---

2. Note that Cyprian raises this anxiety in *On the Lapsed* and *On Works and Almsgiving*, only to decry it; he gives an unequivocal answer, allowing no compromise, whereas Lactantius leaves a certain room for that while driving a similar point (see below).

you walk around laden with booty, wearing spoils, which may incite the minds even of your family. Why do you hesitate to lay out properly something that will be snatched away from you by a single robbery, a sudden proscription, or a raid by an enemy? Why do you fear to make a fragile and perishable good eternal, or to entrust your treasures to God as a guard, in which case you need not fear any thief, robber, decay or tyrant [cf. Luke 12:33–34]? The one who is rich towards God can never be poor [cf. Luke 12:21].

If you value justice so highly, lay aside the burdens that oppress you and follow it; free yourself of fetters and changes that you may run to God unhindered. It is the mark of a great and lofty mind to despise and trample upon mortal affairs. However, if you do not comprehend this virtue, I will free you from fear so that you may offer your wealth to God's altar and provide for yourself more secure possessions than this fragile one. All this instruction is not for you alone but for all the people who are united in mind and hold together as one. If you cannot perform the great deeds alone, cultivate justice as best as you can in such a way that you may excel in other works as much as you excel in the deeds with riches. Do not think that you are being advised to reduce or exhaust your property now, but rather to convert to better uses what you would spend on excesses. Free captives with what you buy wild animals with; support the poor with what you feed those animals with; bury the innocent death with what you buy gladiators with. What does it profit to make rich men out of animal fighters and equip them for crimes? They are wicked anyway. Turn what is about to go to terrible waste to a great sacrifice, so that God will recompense you an eternal gift for these true gifts. Mercy has a great reward; God promises to forgive all sins, saying: "If you hear the prayers of your supplicant, I will hear your prayers; if you have compassion on those in distress, I will have compassion on you in your distress. But if you disregard them or deny help, I will also turn your sympathies against you and will judge you by your laws."[3]

3. The source of this passage is unknown.

7

Basil the Great

Homily 6: "I Will Pull Down My Barns"[1]

1. There are two kinds of temptations. There are afflictions which try the hearts like gold in the furnace, testing their metal by patience. But sometimes—and this is true of many—the very prosperities of life become a temptation. When things go ill, it is hard not to be depressed; when they go too well, it is equally hard not to be puffed up with insolent pride. The first kind of temptation we see in Job, that great and invincible champion; the devil's violence bore down on him like a torrent, but he met it all with unshaken heart and firm purpose; the fiercer and closer his adversary's grip, the greater his triumph proved over his temptations.

Then there is temptation through prosperity, and among examples here is the rich man of our text. He had wealth already; but he hoped for more. God in his mercy did not judge him outright for his ingratitude; rather, God added riches to

---

1. A homily on the parable of the "rich fool" in Luke 12:16–21; the title comes from Luke 12:18. This text and the rest of the selected texts except Homily 7 are my translation.

55

was not moved to generosity

riches, to make the man tire perhaps of plenty and to move his soul to generosity and the common sharing. The Gospel says: "The land of a rich man produced abundantly. And he thought to himself, 'What should I do, for I have no place to store my crops?' Then he said, 'I will do this: I will pull down my barns and build larger ones'" [Luke 12:16–17]. Why was the land left to bring forth in abundance if the man was to put it to no good use? So that God's forbearance should be more evident. Even to people such as this God's goodness is manifest; "he sends his rain on the just and the on the unjust, and makes his sun to rise on the evil and on the good" [cf. Matt 5:45]. But this goodness of God brings greater punishment on the wicked. He sent his showers on the soil, though covetous hands tilled it; he gave his sun to warm the seed and multiply crops with fruitfulness. From God, then, there came these beneficial things—a fit soil, temperate weather, abundant seed, oxen to work with, and all that farming thrives on. And on the human side what was there? Surliness, uncharitableness, selfishness; these were his answer to his Benefactor. He never thought that others were humans as much as he; nor did he think it was his responsibility to distribute his surplus to those in want; he did not heed the commandment: "Do not neglect to do good to the needy" [Prov 3:27 LXX] or "Do not let alms and faithfulness forsake you" [Prov 3:3 LXX]; or "Break your bread for the hungry" [Isa 58:7].

God provided, man was selfish

And all the prophets and all the teachers cried, and they were not heard; his barns groaned with the press of stored harvests, but his miserly heart was not satisfied. He added continually new to old, swelled his plenty with annual increase, and came at length to the hopeless dilemma where greed prevented him from letting the old be brought out, yet he had no room to store the new. Thus his schemes are vain, his cares desperate. "What should I do?" Poor creature, what distress he is in—miserable in his prosperity, pitiable for his present wealth, more pitiable for the greater abundance he expected to receive! The land that should bring him revenue bears lamentations instead; in place of rich harvest, it heaps up troubles

still wasn't satisfied

and cares and utter hopelessness. He complains as the poor do. Will not the destitute, the beggar, utter the selfsame words? "What should I do?" "Where can I find food and clothing?" These are the rich man's words, too. He is broken-spirited, eaten away with care. What heartens others distresses the miser. It does not cheer him to have his granaries filled within; his heart is wrung by the overflow of wealth; he fears it may reach the folk outside and thus help to relieve the destitute.

2. Surely what ails his soul is much what ails the gluttonous, who would burst with cramming rather than give the poor any of their leftovers. Mortal, remember who gives you these goods. And remember yourself—who you are, what you are steward of, from whom you received it, and why you have been favored above most. You have been made the minister of a gracious God, steward for your fellow servants. Do not suppose that all these things were provided for your belly. The wealth you handle belongs to others; think of it accordingly. Not for long will it delight you; soon it will slip from you and be gone, and you will be asked to give strict account of it. Yet you keep it all locked away behind doors and sealed up; and then the thought of it keeps you awake at nights; you take counsel about it inwardly, and your counselor is yourself—a fool! "What should I do?" How easy it would have been to say: "I will fill the souls of the hungry; I will open my barns; I will invite all the poor. I will be like Joseph in his charitable proclamation; I will speak generous words: 'All you who have need of bread, come to me; let each have one's fill from God's bounty, which flows for all'" [cf. Gen 41:53–57]. But that is not your way; no. You begrudge others' satisfaction; you contrive evil schemes within your soul; you are not concerned how to distribute to others according to their needs but how to get everything yourself and keep everyone from using it.

Thus the rich man discoursed on food with his soul, and beside him were those who required his soul. Thus he pictured his enjoyment for many years to come; and that same night he was snatched away. He was permitted to weigh the whole matter, permitted to make his resolve express, so that he might receive a sentence befitting his resolve.

3. See that it goes not so with you. These things have been written that we ourselves may not act in such ways. Imitate the earth; bring forth fruit as it does; should your human status be inferior to a lifeless thing? The earth brings forth fruits not for its own pleasure but for your service; you can reap for yourself the fruit of all generosity because the rewards of good works return to those who offer them. If you give to the hungry, the gift becomes your own and comes back to you with increase. As the wheat falling on the ground brings forth a gain for the one who scatters it, so the grain bestowed on the hungry brings you profit a hundredfold hereafter. Make the end of harvesting the beginning of heavenly sowing, "Sow for yourselves unto justice," the Scripture says [Hos 10:12]. Why then be anxious, why torture yourself, why strive to shut in your riches with bricks and mortar? "A good name is better than great riches" [Prov 22:1]. And if you admire riches for the honor they bring, consider which is more glorious—to be called the father of children innumerable or to have gold coins innumerable in your purse.[2] You must leave your money behind whether you will or not, but your honor coming from the glory of good works will take you to the Master. A whole people, standing around you before their and your Judge, will call you their foster father and benefactor and all the titles gained by charity....

4. The bright gleam of gold delights you; you are heedless of all the lamentation of the needy that rises loud in your wake. How can I bring home to you what the poor man's[3] sufferings are? He casts his eyes round the house, sees that he has no gold and never will have; his clothes and furniture are what the poor's belongings always are—worth a few pennies all together. What then? What is left? He looks at his sons, and thinks he may stave off death by selling them in the market place. Watch the battle between starvation and fatherhood.

2. Basil plays on the words *pater* ("father") and *stater* (a gold coin).
3. Here is a (another) situation where the original language, while still representing the poor in general, seems to come alive and communicate more powerfully in its textual and historical context.

The former threatens him with the most pitiful of deaths, the latter holds him back and bids him die with his children; again and again he starts forward, again and again he checks himself; but the stress of pitiless want is on him, and succumbs at last. And what are his thoughts at such times? "Which should I sell first? Which will please the corn merchant best? Should I take the eldest? He has rights of the firstborn I dare not violate. The youngest then? I pity his youth, still innocent of misery. This one is his parents' living image; this other is ripe for schooling. What hopelessness! What am I to do? Can I turn against any of them? Can I become a brute beast? Can I forget the bond of nature? If I cling to them all, I will see them all wasting away with hunger. If I sacrifice one, with what face can I look at the others? They will suspect me of treachery at once. How can I stay in a household which I myself have orphaned? How can I sit down to my table with food when these are the means of filling it?"

poor man's story... powerful

The poor man goes off in tears to sell his beloved son; but you—you are cold to his misery, you feel no touch of nature. He, poor wretch, is starving; you keep him in suspense, you beat about the bush, drawing out his agony. To keep alive, he offers his own flesh and blood; and you, whose very hand should be stricken with paralysis at receiving the price of such wretchedness, you haggle about the bargain; you try to give less than you get, and in every way you can make the poor creature's burden worse. Tears do not move you, groans do not soften your heart, and you are unrelenting and pitiless. Everything is gold to your eyes and fantasy; gold is your dream at night and your waking care. As a delirious person out of his mind does not see things themselves but imagines things in his diseased fantasy, so your greed-possessed soul sees gold and silver everywhere. Sight of gold is dearer to you than sight of the sun. Your prayer is that everything may be changed to gold, and your schemes are set on brining about gold. . . .

7. "I am not doing wrong to anyone," you say, "I hold fast to my own, that is all." Your own! Who gave it to you to bring into life with you? You are like the one who takes a seat in a

theater and then keeps out newcomers, claiming as his own what is there for the use of everyone. Such are the rich; they seize what belongs to all and claim the right of possession to monopolize it; if everyone took for oneself enough to meet one's own wants and gave up the rest to those who needed it, there would be no rich and no poor. Did you not come naked out of the womb, and will you not go back naked to earth again [cf. Job 1:21]? Whence came the riches you have now? If you say from nowhere, you deny God, you ignore the Creator, and you are ungrateful to the Giver. But if you acknowledge they came from God, tell us the reason why you received them. Is God unjust when he distributes the necessaries of life unequally? Why are you rich and another poor? Surely it is that you may win the reward of generosity and faithful stewardship, and the poor the noble prizes of patience? And yet you store up everything in the pockets of insatiable covetousness and think you wrong no one when you are defrauding so many! Who is a covetous one? One for whom plenty is not enough! Who is the defrauder? One who takes away what belongs to everyone. And are you not covetous, are you not a defrauder, when you keep for private use what you were given for distribution? The person who strips another of clothing is called a thief. And those who might clothe the naked and do not—should they not be given the same name? The bread in your board belongs to the hungry; the cloak in your wardrobe belongs to the naked; the shoes you let rot belong to the barefoot; the money in your vaults belongs to the destitute. All you might help and do not—to all these you are doing wrong.

Homily 7: To the Rich[4]

1. . . . It is thus evident that you are far from fulfilling the commandment, and that you bear false witness within your own soul that you have loved your neighbor as yourself. Look,

---

4. A homily on the rich young man in Matt 19:16–22. Translation of this text comes from C. Paul Schroeder, trans. and intro., *On Social Justice: St. Basil the Great* (Crestwood, NY: St. Vladimir's Seminary Press, 2009), 44–47, 54, 55. Used by permission.

the Lord's offer ["Sell your possessions and give to the poor"] shows just how distant you are from true love! For if what you say is true, that you have kept from your youth the commandment of love and have given to everyone the same as to yourself, then how did you come by this abundance of wealth? Care for the needy requires the expenditure of wealth: when all share alike, disbursing their possessions among themselves, they each receive a small portion for their individual needs. Thus, those who love their neighbor as themselves possess nothing more than their neighbor; yet surely, you seem to have great possessions! How else can this be, but that you have preferred your own enjoyment to the consolation of the many? For the more you abound in wealth, the more you lack in love. . . .

2. After all, what is the use of wealth? Do you wish to wrap yourself in fine apparel? Surely two lengths of cloth are sufficient for a coat, while the covering of a single garment fulfills every need with regard to clothing. Or would you spend your wealth on food? A loaf of bread is enough to fill your stomach. Why then do you grieve? Of what have you been deprived? Of the glory that derives from wealth? Had you not sought glory from the dirt, you would have discovered the true glory like a shining beacon leading you to the kingdom of heaven. Nonetheless, having wealth is dear to you, though you gain from it no advantage whatsoever. And the futility of chasing after what is worthless is obvious to everyone.

Perhaps the lesson of the paradox I am about to speak will be apparent to you; it is, in any case, entirely true. When wealth is scattered in the manner which our Lord directed, it naturally returns, but when it is gathered, it naturally disperses. If you try to keep it, you will not have it; if you scatter it, you will not lose it. "They have distributed freely, they have given to the poor; their righteousness endures forever" [Ps 112:9]. Yet it is not on account of food or clothing that wealth is sought by most. Rather, some device has been concocted by the devil, suggesting innumerable spending opportunities to the wealthy, so that they pursue unnecessary and worthless things as if they were indispensable, and no amount is sufficient for the expenditures they contrive. They divide up their wealth, one part for present needs, and another for the future. They put aside one portion for themselves, and another for their children. Then they distribute their own share among various spending opportunities.

Only listen to the arrangements they make: "There should be," they say, "some wealth for spending, some held in reserve, while the allowance for daily provisions should exceed the level of mere necessities. Some will be for comforts within the house, and some for outward display; some to make traveling comfortable, and some to make life splendid and luxurious at home." I am overwhelmed even at the thought of so many contrived extravagances! There are thousands of carriages, plated with bronze and silver; some carry their owners, while others carry their goods. Multitudes of horses follow, whose lineage can be traced back to noble sires, as if they were human beings. Some bear their masters within the city when they go out for entertainment, some are reserved for hunting, while others are specially groomed for traveling. They wear bridles and belts and garlands all of silver and spangled with gold; they are adorned with blankets of finest purple, arrayed like a bridegroom. Teams of mules, separated according to color, are accompanied by their drivers in successive waves, some going before, others following after. A veritable army of servants is required: butlers, housekeepers, gardeners, master artisans of all kinds, experts at both things needful and those devised purely for pleasure and entertainment: cooks, bakers, wine tasters, hunters, sculptors, painters, specialists in every kind of indulgence. There are caravans of camels, some bearing burdens, others grazing. There are teams of horses, droves of cattle, flocks of sheep, herds of swine with their herdsmen. There are landholdings sufficient to pasture them all, while at the same time increasing the sum of wealth by the revenue they generate. The landowners enjoy baths in the city and in the countryside. Their houses are made with all kinds of translucent marble, some of Phrygian stone, some of Lacaonian or Thessalian tile, which keep them warm in the winter and pleasantly cool in the summer. The floors are decorated with mosaic, the ceilings richly gilt. The portions of the walls that are not tiled are decorated with painted designs.

3. After they have squandered their wealth among so many pursuits, if there is any left over, they hide it in the ground and guard it deep within the earth. "For the future," they say, "is always uncertain; therefore let us take care, lest some unforeseen need should arise." Yet while it is uncertain whether you will have need of this buried gold, the losses you incur from your inhuman behavior are not at all uncertain. When by a multitude of schemes you were unable to exhaust your wealth, you concealed it in the earth. An evident madness! So long as gold remained unearthed in the mines, you scoured the world to find it; but once it came to light, you hid it in the earth again. *ironic* And I think that when it comes to this, as you are burying your wealth, you entomb with it your own heart. "For where you treasure is, there your heart will be also" [Matt 6:21].

This is why the Lord's commands make some sorrowful: *okay* because their lives become unbearable when they are not permitted to indulge in frivolous expenditures. It seems to me that the passion of young man described in the Gospel, and of those like him, may be likened to that of a traveler who hastens to arrive at a famous city, but then stops short and lodges in one of the inns just outside the city walls. By a small degree of laxity, he invalidates all his previous efforts, and deprives himself of beholding the sights of the city. In the same way, there are those who gladly undertake other tasks, but resist laying aside their possessions. I know many who fast, pray, sigh, and demonstrate every manner of piety, so long as it costs them nothing, yet would not part with a penny to help those in distress. Of what profit to them is the remainder of their virtue? The kingdom of heaven does not receive such people, for "it is easier for a camel to go through the eye of a needle than for someone who is rich to enter the kingdom of God" [Matt 19:24].

Although the meaning of our Lord's answer is clear, and he does not lie when he speaks, there are few who are persuaded by it. "How shall we live," someone will say, "when we have renounced everything? What quality of life will there be if everyone sells all and forsakes all?" Do not ask me the rationale behind our Lord's commands. The Lawgiver knows well how to bring what is possible into agreement with the Law. Your heart is tested, as it were, upon the fulcrum of the scale, inclining now towards the true life, now towards present enjoyment. It befits those who possess sound judgment to recognize that they have received wealth as a stewardship, and not for their own enjoyment; thus, when they are parted from it, they rejoice as those who relinquish what is not really theirs, instead of becoming downcast like those who stripped of their own.

Why then are you sad? Why do you mourn in your soul, hearing "Sell your possessions?" Even if your belongings could follow you to the future life, they would not be particularly desirable there, since they would be overshadowed by truly precious things. If, on the other hand, they must remain here, why not sell them now and obtain the profit? You are not disappointed when you must spend gold in order to purchase a horse. But when you have the opportunity to exchange corruptible things for the kingdom of heaven, you shed tears, spurning the One who asks of you and refusing to give anything, while contriving a million excuses for your own expenditures....

7.... "But wealth is necessary for rearing children," someone will say. This is a specious excuse for greed: although you speak as though children were your concern, you betray the inclinations of your own heart. Do not impute guilt to the guiltless! They have their own Master who cares for their needs. They received their being from God, and God will provide what they need to live. Was the command found in the Gospel, "If you wish to be perfect, sell your possessions and give the money to the poor" [Matt 19:21], not written for the married? After seeking the blessing of children from the Lord, and being found worthy to become parents, did you at once add the following, "Give me children, that I might disobey your com-

64

mandments; give me children, that I might not attain the kingdom of heaven?"

Who will vouch for the prudence of your children, that they will use what is left to them for good ends? For many, wealth becomes an aid to immorality. Or do you not hear what is said in Ecclesiastes, "There is a grievous ill that I have seen under the sun: riches were kept by their owners to their hurt" [Eccl 5:13], and moreover, "I will leave that for which I have toiled to those who come after me, and who knows whether they will be wise or foolish" [Eccl 2:18 LXX]? Take care then, lest after countless efforts to acquire riches, you end up providing others with resources to commit sins. In that case, you will find yourself doubly punished, both for acting unjustly in your own right, and for furnishing others with the opportunity to do the same. . . .

8. The foregoing admonitions were given to parents, but what fine-sounding excuse for miserliness will those who have no children produce for themselves? "I do not sell what I have, nor do I give to the poor, because I need what I have to live." Thus, the Lord is not your teacher, nor does the gospel govern your life, but you are a lawgiver unto yourself. See what peril you fall into by thinking this way! If the Lord laid these things down as obligatory, but you write them off as unnecessary, it can only mean that you account yourself wiser than the Lawgiver. Yet you say, "I will enjoy all these things during my life, but after my death I will leave my goods to the poor, making them beneficiaries of my will and granting them all my possessions." When you are no longer among your fellow human beings, then you will become a philanthropist!

Homily 8: In Time of Famine and Drought

2. . . . . We know that the Lord sent us all these calamities as a result of our turning away from him and being negligent in his service, not in order to exterminate us but to correct us like our good parents, concerned about the welfare of their children; they become angry against their children and punish

65

them, not because they desire to do them harm, but because they want to correct their youthful carelessness and to draw them away from their sinful ways and back to the path of virtue.

What then, is the cause of such disorder and confusion? What is the reason for the strange new manifestation in the nature in these days? Let us investigate this, since we are endowed with reason; let us reason, since we are rational beings. Is it because there is not one to govern the universe? Is it because God, the Master Artisan, has neglected his created order? Is it because he has lost all power and authority?

No, the reason why we are not governed in the usual way is clear and self-evident: We receive, but give to nobody; we praise good works, but do not practice them towards the needy. We were slaves, and we have been set free, and yet we do not have sympathy for those who, like ourselves, are slaves of the Lord. When we are hungry, we eat, and yet we close our eyes to those who are needy. We have God as our unfailing provider and dispenser, and yet we have shown ourselves stingy and close-fisted towards the poor. Our sheep have produced numerous lambs, and yet the poor are more numerous than our sheep. Our barns and granaries are too tight for what we store in them, and yet we ourselves do not have compassion for those who suffer from tight circumstances. For all these things we are threatened with righteous judgment. If God does not open his hands for us, it is because we have cast out love for our brothers and sisters. For this reason, the farmlands are dry....

7. The pain of starvation, from which the hungry die, is a horrible suffering. Of all human calamities, famine is the principal one; and the most miserable of deaths is, no doubt that by starvation. When considering other kinds of death, the sword puts a quick end to life; the roaring fire too quickly burns out the sap of life; even the teeth of wild animals, mangling the vital limbs, would not prolong the torture. But famine is a slow torture which prolongs the pain; it is an infirmity well established and hidden in its place, a death always present and

never coming to an end. It dries up the bodily liquids, diminishes the body heat, contracts the size, and little by little drains off the strength. The flesh clings to the bones like a cobweb. The skin has no color. . . . The belly is hollow, contracted, formless, without weight, without the natural stretching of the viscera, joined to the bones of the back. Now, what punishment should not be inflicted upon the one who passes by such a body? What cruelty can surpass that? How can we not count someone like that among the fiercest of beasts and consider that person as a sacrilegious one and a murderer? The person who can cure such an infirmity and refuses one's medicine because of avarice, can with reason be condemned as a murderer.

keep-
murderer

Homily on Psalm 14[5]: Against Lending with Interest

1. . . . In many passages of the Scripture, lending with interest in condemned as sinful. Thus Ezekiel places taking interest among the major evils [Ezek 22:12] and the law clearly forbids it: "You shall not demand interest from your brother and your neighbor" [Deut 23:20 LXX]. Elsewhere it is said: "Deceit upon deceit, usury upon usury" [Jer 9:6 LXX]. And of the city that prospers on a multitude of sins, it is said in the Psalm: "Usury and fraud never part from its streets" [Ps 54:12 LXX]. The prophet [David], pointing out something as the mark or seal of human perfection, also says: "He never lends his money for interest" [Ps 14:5 LXX]. Indeed, it is extremely inhuman that some have to beg for the most basic necessities to support their lives while others are not satisfied with the capital they have, but excogitate ways of increasing their opulence at the expense of the poor in distress. . . .

inhuman

5. You rich, listen to the advice that we give to the poor in view of your inhumanity: Bear any suffering rather than the calamities that will come from usury. But if you obey the Lord, there will be no need for such an advice. Now what does the Lord advise? "Lend to those from whom there is no hope

5. LXX. It is Psalm 15 in contemporary versions of the Christian Old Testament.

of repayment" [Luke 6:35]. But, you say, how can it be called "lending" if there is no hope of repayment? Try to understand the meaning of the Lord's saying and you will admire the goodness of that law. When you give to the poor for the love of God, the same thing is both gift and loan. Gift, first, because there is no hope of receiving anything in return; loan, secondly, because the Lord will reward you abundantly through the poor and because for such a trifle that you give to them, you will receive huge sums in return.

Thus "whoever gives alms to the poor lends to God" [Prov 19:17]. Would you not hold the Lord of the universe as your debtor who is obliged to repay? Would you accept the warranty of a rich man in the city who receives the payment of others and not that of God who will pay abundantly through the poor? Give your surplus money, do not burden it with interest, and both you and your debtor will fare well. You will keep your money secure; the other who receives it, will derive benefit from its use. But if you look for interest, be satisfied with those given by the Lord. He will pay, through the poor, the due interest. From the One who is true lover of humanity, it is good that you expect payment worthy of his love.

If you take from the poor, you commit the worst crime of inhumanity: you derive profit from miseries, you gain money from tears, you oppress the needy, you starve the hungry. You have no mercy whatsoever, you do not realize the bond you have with those who suffer. And yet you call acts of humanity the profits you receive. "Woe to those who call evil good, and good evil, who change darkness into light, and light into darkness, and change bitter into sweet, and sweet into bitter" [Isa 5:20] and those who give the name of philanthropy to misanthropy.

The Shorter Rules, Question 92

Question 92: Since the Lord commanded us to sell all our possessions [Luke 12:33],[6] on what understanding or basis should

6. Cf. Matt 19:21; Mark 10:21; Luke 18:22.

we do this? Is it because the goods are in themselves condemnable or because they cause distractions to the soul?

Answer: To this question it may be answered first that if the goods were bad in themselves, then they could have in no way been created by God. For "everything God created is good; nothing is to be rejected" [1 Tim 4:4]. Secondly, the Lord's command does not teach that we have to reject and flee possessions as though they are bad, but that we should administer them. And the ones who are condemned are condemned not because they possess things, but because they make a bad use of what they possess. Therefore, a detached attitude towards and a sound respect for the earthly goods and a wise administration of them according to the command of the Lord are of great help in obtaining many things. First, to purify us of our sins, as it is written, "But give as alms those things which are within; and behold all things are pure for you" [Luke 11:41]; and secondly, to gain the kingdom of heaven and possess an inexhaustible treasure.... "Fear not little flock, for it is your heavenly Father's good pleasure to give you the kingdom. Sell your possessions and give alms. Make for yourselves purses which do not wear out, a treasure in the heavens that does not fail" [Luke 12:32–33].

8

Gregory of Nyssa

On the Love of the Poor 1[1]

... There is an abstinence which is not bodily, a spiritual self-discipline which affects the soul; this is abstinence from evil, and it was as a means to this that our abstinence from food was prescribed. Therefore I say to you: Fast from evil-doing; discipline yourselves from covetousness; abstain from unjust profits; starve your greed for mammon, keep in your houses no snatched and stolen treasure. What use is it to keep meat out of your mouth if you wound your brother or sister by evil doing? What advantage is it to forgo what is your own if you seize unjustly what belongs to the poor? What piety is it to drink water and thirst for blood, weaving treachery in the wicked-ness of your heart? Judas himself fasted with the eleven, but since he did not curb his love for money, his fasting availed him

---

1. Based on the Greek text I have revised and expanded Peter C. Phan's translation in
   Social Thought (Message of the Fathers of the Church 20; Wilmington, DE: Glazier, 1984).
   Used by permission.

nothing to salvation. The devil does not eat since he is an incorporeal spirit, but he fell from on high through wickedness.

If we bear ourselves no better than this, Isaiah will say to us: "Why do you fast for strife and contention, and strike the hungry with your fists" [Isa 58:4]? Let Isaiah too set forth the actions of a pure and sincere fast: "Loosen every bond of injustice, set the oppressed free, untie the knots of covenants made by force. Share your bread with the hungry; bring the poor and homeless into your house. When you see the naked, cover them; and do not despise your own flesh" [Isa 56:6–7]. These days have brought us naked and homeless people in great number; a host of captives is at everyone's door; strangers and refugees are not lacking, and on every side their begging and stretched-out hands are there to see. Their house is the open air; their lodgings are the arcades, the streets, the deserted corners of the market; they lurk in holes like owls and birds of the night. Their clothing is tattered rags; their means of subsistence depends on the feeling of human compassion. Their food is anything thrown by the passers-by; their drink is the springs they share with the animals. . . . They live a brutal and vagrant life, not by habit but as a result of their miseries and misfortunes.

You who are fasting, these are the people I charge you to help. Be generous to these, your distressed brothers and sisters. Give to the hungry what you deny to your own appetite. Let the fear of God even out the differences between you and them. With self-control, avoid two contrary evils: your own gluttony and the hunger of your brothers and sisters. . . . Grab the afflicted one as gold. Take the sufferer to your arms as you would your own health, as you would look after the welfare of your wife, children, servants and all your house. A poor person who is sick is doubly in need. The poor who are in good health can pass from door to door; they can go in search of the well-to-do; they can sit at the crossroads and cry out to all who pass by. But people shackled by illness, people cooped up in some narrow lodging-place or corner like Daniel in the den[2], these

---

2. Dan 14:33–39 Vulgate; Bel and the Dragon 31–42.

wait for you—the devout one, the friend of the poor—as though for Habakkuk.

But you will say: "I am poor as well." Granted, suppose you are. Nevertheless, give what you can; God asks for nothing beyond your means. You can give bread, someone else will give a cup of wine, another clothing; in this way, one person's hardship will be relieved by your combined contribution. Moses did not take the offerings for the tabernacle from one benefactor but from the whole people; the rich brought gold, another silver; the poor brought animal skins, and one still poorer the hair of goats. Consider, too, how the widow's mite was more than the offerings of the rich; she gave everything she had; the rich threw in only a portion of what they had [Luke 21:1–4].

Do not despise these people in their abjection; do not think they merit no respect. Reflect on who they are and you will understand their dignity; they have taken upon them the person of our Savior. For he, the compassionate, has given them his own person in order to shame the unmerciful and the haters of the poor—just as people lift up images of the emperor against those who would do them violence, putting their despisers to shame by the likeness of the prince. The poor are the treasurers of the good things that we look for, the doorkeepers of the kingdom, opening its gates to the merciful and shutting them on the harsh and uncharitable. They are the strongest of accusers, the best of defenders—not that they accuse or defend in words, but that the Lord beholds what is done towards them, and every deed cries louder to him who searches all hearts than the herald's trumpet.

God himself is the prime author of beneficence, the rich and generous provider of all that we need. But we, who are taught in every letter of the Scripture to imitate our Lord and Maker—as much as the mortal may imitate the divine and immortal—we snatch everything to our own enjoyment, assigning some things to ourselves to live upon, hoarding the rest for our heirs. Merciless as we are, we care nothing for the unfortunate, we give no kindly thought to the poor. We see a fellow human with no bread to eat, no food to sustain life itself;

yet far from hastening to help, far from offering that person a rescue, we leave him like a once sturdy plant to wither unwatered pitifully away under a scorching sun—and this even if we have wealth to overflowing and might let the channels of our abundance run forth to comfort many. The flow from one river-source brings richness to many a spreading plain; so the wealth of one household is enough to preserve multitudes of the poor, if only a grudging uncharitable heart does not fall like a stone to block the passage and hinder the stream.

You, therefore, who have been created rational beings, endowed with mind to expound and interpret divine things, do not be enticed by what is only transitory. Strive to win those things which never forsake their holder. Live with restraint; do not think everything your own, but reserve a part for God's dear poor. All things belong to God, our common Father. We are all of the same stock, all brothers and sisters. And when people are siblings, the best and most equitable thing is that they should inherit in equal portions. The second best is that even if one or two take the greater part, the others should have at least their own share. But if one man should seek to be absolute possessor of all, refusing even a third or a fifth to his siblings, then he is a cruel tyrant, a savage with whom there can be no dealing, an insatiate beast gloatingly shutting its jaws over the meal it will not share. Or rather he is more ruthless than any beast; wolf does not drive wolf from the prey, and a pack of dogs will tear the same carcass; this man in his insatiable greed will not admit one fellow creature to a share in his riches.

Let us then, as rational beings, consider how fleeting our life is; like the waters of a river, time flows ceaselessly and irresistibly on, sweeping everything in its path to the end, which is death. It is short-lived and brings us no security; would that it brought no reckoning either! But the grave thing is that for every hour we live, every word we say, we must make our defense at an incorruptible tribunal. Therefore the blessed psalmist meditates such things and desires to know his own moment of death. He implores God that he may learn the number of his remaining days as to prepare for his final moment —not confounded like some unready traveler who must seek for the necessities of his journey after he is already on his way. He says therefore: "O Lord, make me know my end and what is the measure of my days, that I may learn what is lacking to me. Behold, you have made my days as it were a handbreadth, and my time is as nothing before you" [Ps 39:4–5]. See the wise care of a prudent soul, even in the royal rank.[3] He views the King of kings and the Judge of judges as clearly in a glass, and he desires to order his living to the perfect pattern of the commandments here, then to depart from here as a true citizen of the life there. May we all attain it also, by the grace and compassion of Jesus Christ our Lord, to whom be glory forever and ever. Amen.

---

3. Referring to king David the psalmist.

9

Gregory of Nazianzus

Oration 14: On the Love of the Poor[1]

4. Solitude and silence are a good thing; this is the lesson I draw from Elijah's Carmel, John's desert, or Jesus's mountain, to which he has often retreated, to be by himself in silence and peace. Simplicity is a good thing; this is the lesson I draw from Elijah, who visited at a widow's house, and from John, who was cloaked in camel's hair, and from Peter, who fed himself on a few bits of lupines. Humility is a good thing, and there are many examples of this on various sides; chief among them is the Savior and Lord of all, who not only humbled himself as far as taking "the form of a slave" [Phil 2:6] or simply submit his face to the shame of being spat upon, and let himself be "numbered with transgressors" [Isa 50:6; 53:12; Luke 22:37]—he who purged the world of sin—but who also washed the feet of his disciples dressed as a slave. Poverty and contempt for worldly goods are a good thing, as exemplified by

---

1. My translation.

Zacchaeus and Christ himself: the former, by putting almost all his wealth at the disposal of others when Christ visited his house [Luke 19:8], the latter by defining perfection in these very terms when he spoke with the rich man [Matt 19:21]. To put it still more succinctly concerning all these virtues, contemplation is a good thing, and action is also a good thing: the first, because it raises us up and leads us to the Holy of Holies, conducting our mind upwards towards what is akin to it; the second, because it receives Christ as its guest and cares for him, revealing the power of love by its good works.

5. Each of these virtues is one path to salvation, and certainly leads towards one of the blessed, eternal dwellings; just as there are many different chosen forms of life, so there are many rooms in God's house [John 14:2], assigned and distributed to each person according to individual merit. So one person may cultivate this virtue, the other that, another several, still another all of them—if that is possible! Let each one simply walk on the way, press forward, and follow the footsteps of the One who leads the way, with good guidance and direction, through the narrow path and gate to the broad plains of heavenly bliss. And if, following the command of Paul and of Christ himself, we must regard that love is the first and greatest of the commandments, the sum of the law and the prophets [Matt 22:26], I must conclude that love of the poor, and compassion and sympathy for our own flesh and blood, is its most excellent form. No better sacrifice can be offered to God than mercy, since no other thing is more proper to God, before whom mercy and truth march [Ps 89:14 (88:14 LXX)] and to whom mercy is to be offered rather than condemnation. And God, who makes just recompense and weighs our mercy with his balance and scales, will repay human kindness with the same kindness.

6. We must open our hearts, then, to all the poor and all the victims of disasters from whatever cause, for the Scripture commands us to "rejoice with those who rejoice and weep with those who weep" [Rom 12:15]. Simply because we are human beings, we must offer the gift of our kindness to all other

human beings: whether they need it because they are widows or orphans; or because they are exiles (refugees) from their own country; or because of the cruelty of their masters, the ruthlessness of their rulers, or the inhumanity of their tax-collectors; or because of the brutality of robbers or the insatiable greed of thieves; or because of the legal confiscation of their property, or shipwreck. All are wretched and miserable alike and look towards our hands, in the same way as we look towards God's hands for our own needs. But of all these groups, those who suffer evil and calamities in a way that contradict their former dignity and standing are even more wretched than those who are used to misfortune. Especially, then, we must open our hearts to those infected by the "sacred disease" [i.e., leprosy], who are being consumed even in their flesh and bones and marrow—the disease that Scripture threatens against some individuals [cf. Isa 10:16–18; Ps 38:3]. . . .

8. . . . We must, each of us, care no less for the physical needs of our neighbors than our own, the bodies both of the healthy and of those consumed by this disease [leprosy]. For we are all one in the Lord, rich or poor, slave or free [Rom 12:5], healthy or sick in body; and there is one head of all, Christ, from whom all things proceed. What the limbs are to each other, each of us is to everyone else, and all to all. This is why we must not overlook or neglect to care for those who experience our common infirmity before we do; nor should we delight more in the fact that we enjoy bodily well-being than we grieve that our brothers and sisters are in misery. Rather, we must believe this to be the single way towards the salvation both of our bodies and of our souls: loving compassion [*pilanthrōpia*] shown towards our fellow humans.

9. For most people, one thing alone causes misery: a lack of material resources. Perhaps time, or hard work, or a friend, or a relative, the passing of time, or a change in circumstances might take it away. But for these people [i.e., people with leprosy], misery is augmented even more abundantly, in that they are deprived of the resources to work and to help themselves acquire the necessities of life because of their flesh; and the

fear of growing weaker always outweighs any hope of recovery. As a result, they find little support in hope, which is the only antidote that really helps the unfortunate. In addition to their poverty, they are afflicted with a second evil, disease: the most oppressive and horrendous evil of all and thus the one that many would call a curse! And a third evil for them is the fact that most people will not approach them, or look at them, that all run away from them, and find them disgusting and abominable. This is something that preys on them even more than the disease: to perceive that they are actually hated because of their misfortune. I cannot bear to think about their suffering without tears, and I am overwhelmed when I recall them; I hope you feel the same way yourselves, that you might put their tears to flight with your tears. I am sure that those among you who love Christ and love the poor feel this way; for it is God who has given you a capacity for compassion and you give witness to your feelings yourselves. . . .

16. [T]hey live their wretched lives under the open sky, while we live in splendid homes, decked out with stones of every color, gleaming with gold and silver and delicate mosaic and fresco that charm and beguile the eyes! We live in some of these houses; we are building others, but for whom? Perhaps not even for our heirs, but for strangers and foreigners, or even for those who do not like us, I suppose, but—worst of all—our bitter and hostile enemies! These people shiver in worn and tattered rags—if they are so fortunate to have even those —while we pamper ourselves with soft, flowing robes and exquisite garments of linen and silk that seem to exhibit more of our disorder than dignity; we store away our clothes in chests—a useless and unprofitable provision—as food for the moths and for all consuming time. These people lack the most basic nourishment (how can I be so self-indulgent, while they are bemoaning their misfortune?), but lie before our doorways, faint and famished, not even possessing any bodily strength to beg; they have no voice to cry out in pain, no hands to stretch out in supplication, no feet to approach the wealthy, no noses to give resonance to their complaints; and, regarding

this heaviest of all burdens to be lightest, they feel grateful to their eyes, because they are spared the sight of their own mutilation. . . .

18. What are we to make of all this, my friends, my brothers and sisters? Why are we ourselves sick in our very souls, with a sickness much more serious than that of the body? It is clear to us that the bodily sickness is involuntary but the spiritual sickness comes from our choice; while the one ends with this life, the other accompanies us when we are brought to the next; while the one deserves compassion, the other, hatred, at least on the part of those with sound mind. Why do we not assist our own natural kin, while we have time? Why do we not attempt to help them in the lowly state of their flesh, even as we are flesh ourselves? Why do we revel in the midst of our brothers' and sisters' misfortunes? May God preserve me—from being rich while they are destitute, from being in good health if I do not tend their wounds, from having enough food or clothing, and from resting in my home, if I do not offer them bread, give them something to wear, and welcome them into my home, as far as I can! Either we must give everything away for Christ's sake, so that we may become his true followers, taking up our cross; so that we might confidently soar towards the world on high, well equipped and unencumbered; so that we might gain Christ at the cost of everything else, exalted through humility and made rich by our poverty. Or we must share our goods with Christ, so that our possession of them may at least be made holy by our possessing them well, by sharing them with those who have nothing. Even if I were to sow for myself alone, I would still be sowing what others would later eat. To quote the words of Job again, "Instead of wheat, nettles would come forth, and instead of barley, brambles" [Job 31:40]; a searing wind would appear, and a violent storm would destroy my efforts, so that I would have toiled in vain. And even if I were to build barns and store up wealth upon wealth, this very night I would be asked for my soul and must give account for the treasures I unjustly laid up [cf. Luke 12:20]. . . .

22. Therefore, let us now follow the Word. Let us seek our

rest in the world to come, and cast aside our surplus posses-sions in this world. Let us only hold on to what is good from all these things: let us gain our souls by acts of mercy; let us share what we have with the poor so that we may be rich in the abundance of heaven. Give a portion of your goods to your soul, not just to your body; give a portion to God, not just to the world. Take something away from the belly and consecrate it to the spirit. Snatch something from the fire, store it far from the consuming flame from below. Seize it from the tyrant, and entrust it to the Lord. Give a portion to the "seven"—that is, to this life—and also to the "eight"—to the life that will receive us after this.[2] Give a little to him from whom you have received much; even give your all to the One who has given all to you. You will never surpass God's bountiful generosity, even if you hand over your entire property and yourself in the bargain. Indeed, to receive in the truest sense is to be given to God! However much you contribute, there is always more left over; and you are never giving away what is your own, since all things come from God. Just as it is impossible to step over our own shadow, which moves along exactly as far as we do, and always reaches out the same distance before us—just as the height of a body cannot exceed the head, since the head is always above the body—so, too, it is impossible to surpass God in our giving. For we never give him anything that does not belongs to him or that outshines his munificence. . . .

25. Let us keep the supreme and first law of God, who sends rain on the just and the sinners, and makes the sun rise equally on all [Matt 5:45]. He has spread out the unoccupied land for everyone on earth, with springs and rivers and forests; he has given air for the winged species, and water for all aquatic crea-tures; he generously provides the basic elements of life to all without subjecting them to any power of force, any limits of law, or any divisions of geographical boundaries. No, he has set

2. Eccl 11:2 LXX: "Give a portion to the seven, and indeed to the eight." As Brian Daley notes, "Gregory apparently takes the number 'seven' here to refer to life in this world, created in seven days, and 'eight' to refer to the new creation, beginning with God's 'eighth day' of resurrection" (*Gregory of Nazianzus* [The Early Church Fathers; New York: Routledge, 2006], 216).

forth all of the same necessities as the common possessions of all, so that no one would lack anything. In this way, he honors the equality of nature by the equality of the gifts, and displays the abundance of his goodness. But human beings, in contrast, bury gold and silver and soft, superfluous clothing in the ground, as well as their glittering jewels and other similar kind, which bear the signs of war and discord and the first act of rebellion; they then raise their eyebrows in perplexity and refuse to show mercy to the unfortunate who are their natural kin. They neither wish to help those in need out of their surplus—what perversity! what foolishness!—nor do they even consider this fact: that what we call poverty and wealth, freedom and slavery, and other, similar names, were introduced into human history at a later stage as a sort of epidemics that assault us accompanying sin, and is a symptom of it. But, as Scriptures says, "from the beginning it was not so" [Matt 19:8]. The One who created the human person in the beginning made him free and endowed him with free will, subject only to the law of his commandment, and rich in the delights of Paradise. And God desired to bestow the same freedom on the rest of the human race, through the single seed of the first common ancestor. Freedom and wealth consisted simply in keeping the commandment, whereas true poverty and slavery came from its transgression.

26. But since then, envy and dissensions have infected our lives, and the treacherous tyranny of the serpent constantly seduces us with lust for pleasure and provokes the more powerful against the weaker; our human family has been fragmented into multiple groups, and greed has destroyed the nobility of our nature, even to the extent of controlling the law, the proxy of political power. But look, I ask you, to humanity's original equality, not to its later distinction; not to the law of the tyrant, but to that of Creator. As far as you can, support nature, honor the original freedom, respect yourself, cover the shame of our race, assist those with sickness, and aid those in need. Let the healthy help the sick, and the rich assist the poor; let those who have not stumbled raise up those who lie fallen

and afflicted; let those in good spirits comfort the discouraged, those who enjoy prosperity, support those who labor in adversity. Give thanks to God that you are among those who can do favors for others, rather than among those who need receive them; that you do not look to the hands of others for help, but others to yours. Grow rich not only in wealth but also in piety, not only with your gold but also with your virtue—or better still, only with this! Become more prominent than your neighbor by proving yourself more generous; become a god to the unfortunate by imitating God's mercy. . . .

39. I am also encouraged by Christ's money box, which urge us to care for the poor; and the agreement of Peter and Paul, who, while dividing up the preaching of the Gospel [between Jews and Gentiles], made the poor their common concern [Gal 2:8-10]; and the way of perfection of the young man, defined by the law of giving one's possessions to the poor [Matt 19:21]. Do you think that kindness to your neighbor is not an obligation upon you, but a matter of choice? Not a law, but merely an exhortation? I wish that this were so very much myself, but I am terrified by the goats summoned by the sovereign Judge to be on his left hand with his rebukes against them [see Matt 25:31-46]. They are condemned to be put on that side, not because they have committed theft, sacrilege, or adultery, or have done something else forbidden, but because they have not cared for Christ in the person of the poor!

40. If at all you believe in what I say, then, servants, brothers and sisters and fellow heirs of Christ, while there is still time, let us visit Christ; let us take care of Christ's needs, let us feed Christ, let us clothe Christ, let us welcome Christ, let us honor Christ—not just inviting him to our tables, as some did, nor just with ointment, like Mary, nor just with a tomb, like Joseph of Arimathea; nor just with the things needed for burial, like Nicodemus who loved Christ only half-heartedly; nor just with gold, frankincense and myrrh, like the Magi who visited him before all the rest. But since the Lord of all "desires mercy and not sacrifice" [Hos 6:6; cf. Matt 9:13], and since "a compassionate heart is worth more than thousands of fat sheep" [Dan 3:39

LXX], let us give this gift to him through the needy, who are downtrodden today, so that when we depart from this place, they may receive us into the eternal habitations [cf. Luke 16:9] in Christ himself, who is our Lord, to whom be glory for ever and ever. Amen.

10

John Chrysostom

Homilies on the Rich Man and Lazarus[1]

2.4. . . . Strictly speaking, the rich man [Luke 16:19–31] has not committed an act of injustice against Lazarus, since he did not rob him of his possessions. His sin consisted rather in not giving part of his own possessions. Now if the one who does not give part of his possessions is prosecuted by the one whom he did not pity, what forgiveness can he obtain who steals possessions of others, since those whom he has oppressed will encircle him on all sides? He will need no witnesses, no prosecutors, no proofs, no evidence—but the facts themselves, as they appear before our eyes. "People and their works will appear before me," says the Lord.

Thus, not giving part of one's possessions to others is already a kind of robbery. If what I am telling you sounds perhaps rather odd, do not be surprised. I will present a text from

Robbery

---

1. Based on the Greek texts I have revised and expanded Peter C. Phan's translation in *Social Thought* (Message of the Fathers of the Church 20; Wilmington, DE: Glazier, 1984). Used by permission.

the divine Scriptures which says that it is rapine, avarice, and theft, not only taking possession of things belonging to others but also refusing to give part of one's possessions to others. What text is this? Reproaching the Jews through the mouth of the prophet, God says: "The earth has produced its fruits but you have not brought in tithes, and robbery of the poor dwells in your house" [Mal 3:10]. "Because you have made the customary offerings," says the Lord, "you have taken away what belongs to the poor." He says this in order to make it clear to the rich that what they possess belongs to the poor, even when they receive the inheritance from their parents or come in for some money, whatever the source. Elsewhere God also says: "Do not rob the poor man of his livelihood" [Sir 4:1]. A robbery is taking and keeping what is not one's own. These texts therefore teach that if we refuse to give alms, we will be punished in the same way as robbers.

To the People of Antioch

2.6. . . . . What does the Apostle mean when he says that "God provides us richly with all things for our use" [1 Tim 6:17]? God gives us abundantly all things that are much more necessary than money, such as air, water, fire, sunshine and things of this kind. And yet it cannot be said that the rich have more sunshine than the poor, nor can it be said that the rich breathe more air than the poor. All these things are available to all, equally and in common. Why is it that the greatest and most necessary things, things that sustain our life, have been created by God for common use, and the least and most sordid thing, namely money, is not common? Why? I would like to ask. That is to safeguard our life and to open for us a path to virtue. On the one hand, if the necessities of life were not common, the rich, with their usual greediness, would perhaps take them away from the poor. In fact, if they have done so with money, how much more would they do with these things? On the other hand, if money were common and were available to all, then there would be no opportunity for almsgiving and no incentive for charity.

Homilies on the Gospel of Matthew

5.8. . . . When [Christ] said, "Make to yourselves friends," he did not just stop at this, but added, "of the unrighteous mammon" [Luke 16:9], so that again the good work may be your own; for he has signified here nothing else but almsgiving. And, what is marvelous, neither does he make a strict account with us if we withdraw ourselves from injustice. What he says is like this: "Have you gained ill? Spend well. Have you gathered riches by unrighteousness? Scatter them abroad in righteousness." But what kind of virtue is this, to give out of such gains? God, however, being full of love to humanity, condescends even to this and if we do in this way, promises us many good things; but while plundering without end, if we contribute the smallest part, we think we have fulfilled all. Have you not heard Paul saying, "The one who sows sparingly, will reap also sparingly" [2 Cor 9:6]? . . .

9. Disperse, therefore, that you may not lose; do not keep, that you may keep; lay out, that you may save; spend, that you may gain. If your treasures are to be hoarded, do not hoard them yourself, for you will surely throw them away; entrust them rather to God, then no one can make spoil of them. . . . Lend, where there is no envy, no accusation, nor evil design, nor fear. Lend to the One who wants nothing, yet has need for your sake; who feeds all people, yet is hungry so that you may not suffer famine; who is poor so that you may be rich. Lend there where your return cannot be death, but life instead of death. This usury is the harbinger of a kingdom of hell; the one coming of covetousness, the other of self-denial; the one of cruelty, the other of humanity. What excuse then will be ours, when having the power to receive more, and that with security, and in due season, and in great freedom, without reproaches, fears, or dangers, we let go these gains, and follow after other sorts of "gains," base and wicked as they are, inse-

cure and perishable, and greatly aggravating the furnace for us?

For nothing is baser, nothing is more cruel than the interest that comes from lending. For such lenders trade on other persons' calamities, draw profit from the distress of others, and demand wages for kindness, as though they were afraid to look merciful. Under the mask of kindness the lenders dig deeper the grave of poverty; when they stretch out their hand to help, they push the afflicted down; and when the former receives the latter as it were in a harbor, they involve the afflicted in shipwrecks as on a rock, or shoal, or reef.

Now the usurer will tell me: "Are you asking me to give others for their use the money that I have got together, and which is useful to me, and demand no reward?" No, I am not saying this. On the contrary, I do want that you should receive a reward; not however a mean nor small one, but far greater; for in return for gold, I want you to receive heaven for interest. Why then shut yourself up in poverty, crawling about the earth, and demanding little for great? This is the lot of those who do not know how to be rich. When God in return for a little money is promising you the good things that are in heaven, you say: "Don't give me heaven, but instead of heaven, give me the gold that perishes." This is for one who wishes to continue to live in poverty. Even as one who surely desires wealth and abundance will choose things lasting rather than things perishing, the inexhaustible, rather than that wastes away, much rather than little, the incorruptible rather then the corruptible, so the other sort too will follow. As those who seek earth before heaven will surely lose early also, so those who prefer heaven to earth, will enjoy both in great excellency. Since this may be the case with us, let us despise all things here, and choose the good things to come. We will thus obtain both the one and the other, by the grace and love toward humanity of our Lord Jesus Christ. . . .

12.5. . . . . Is it not the highest form of folly to heap up all your possessions where destruction and waste is the lot of all that is stored, but where things abide untouched and increase, there not to lay up even the least portion, and this, when we are to live there for all eternity? This is the reason why the pagans do not believe what we say. Our actions and our works are the demonstrations which they are willing to receive from us; but when they see us building for ourselves fine houses, and laying out gardens and baths, and buying fields, they are not willing to believe that we are preparing for another sort of residence away from our city.

"If this were so," they would say, "they [Christians] would sell everything they have and deposit the money there beforehand." This is what they conjecture from the way things are usually done in this life. We see indeed that this is what those who are very rich do: they get themselves houses and fields and all the rest, chiefly in those cities in which they are to stay. But we do just the opposite; with all earnest zeal we get possession of the earth, which we are soon to leave; for a few acres and tenements we give up not only money but even our very blood; while for the purchase of heaven we do not endure to give even what is beyond our wants, and this though we are to purchase it at a small price, and to possess it forever, provided we had once purchased it.

Therefore I say we will have to leave this world naked and poor, and suffer the utmost punishment. And we will suffer not only for our own poverty, but also for our making others to be such as ourselves. When pagans see those who have partaken of so great mysteries earnest about these matters, much more will they cling to the things present, heaping fire upon our head. When we, who ought to teach them to despise all things visible, do ourselves especially urge them to the lust of these things, when will it be possible for us to be saved, having to give an account for the destruction of others? Do you not hear Christ say that he left us to be salt and light in the world [cf. Matt 5:13–14], so that we may both brace up those who are melting in luxury, and enlighten them who are darkened by the care of wealth? Therefore, when we even throw them into more thorough darkness, and make them more licentious, what hope will we have for salvation? There is none at all but only wailing and gnashing our teeth; and bound hand and foot, we will depart into the fire of hell, after being fully well-worn down by the cares of riches.

Considering all these things then, let us loose the bands of such deceit, that we may not at all fall into those things that deliver us over to the unquenchable fire. Those who are slaves to money, the chains both here and there will keep them continually bound; but those who rid of this desire will gain freedom from both. To what we also may attain, let us break in pieces the grievous yoke of avarice, and make ourselves wings toward heaven. . . .

49.4. The temporal goods are but an appendage to the spiritual ones; they are so vile and trifling in comparison with these, however great they may be. Let us not therefore spend our energies on them, but regard their acquisition and loss with equal indifference, like Job who neither clung to them when present, nor sought them absent. On this account riches are called *chrēmata* [utilities], so that we should not bury them in the earth but should use them rightly. Each artisan has one's peculiar skill, so does the rich. The rich do not know how to work in brass, nor to frame ships, nor to weave, nor to build houses, nor any such thing. Then, let them learn to use their wealth rightly, and to have mercy on the poor; so will they know a better art than all those.

Truly this is the highest of arts. Its workshop is built in heaven. Its tools are not made of iron and brass, but of goodness and right will. Of this art Christ and his Father are the Teachers. "Be merciful," says he, "as your Father who is in heaven" [Luke 6:36]. And what is indeed marvelous, being so superior to the rest, is that it needs no labor, no time for its perfection; it is enough to have willed, and the whole is accomplished. But let us see also its end, what it is. What then is the end of it? Heaven, the good things in the heavens, that ineffable glory, the spiritual bride-chambers, the bright lamps, the abiding with the Bridegroom, and other things, which no speech or even understanding, is able to express. Herein lies the immense difference between this art and the others. Most of the arts profit us for the present life, whereas this for the life to come also. . . .

52.4. . . . Therefore the rich will justly, proving that they are wicked, be more punished than the poor, since they were not softened even by their prosperity. Don't tell me that they gave alms, since if they did not give in proportion to their fortune, they will not escape punishment. Our alms are judged not by the measure of our gifts, but by the largeness of our heart. But if these suffer punishment, much more will those who are eager about superfluous things; who build houses of two or three stories, but despise the hungry; who give heed to covetousness, but neglect almsgiving. . . .

5. . . . Almsgiving is an art and better than all arts. If the peculiarity of art is to issue in something useful, and nothing is more useful than almsgiving, it is obvious that this is both an art and better than all arts. For it makes for us not shoes, nor does it weave garments, nor build houses of clay; but it procures life everlasting, snatches us from the hands of death, in either life shows us glorious, and builds the mansions that are in heaven and those eternal tabernacles. . . .

Indeed of the arts of this life, each has and realizes one object only. Agriculture, for example, feeds us; weaving clothes us; or rather not so much as this, for each of them is in no way sufficient by itself to contribute to us its own part. Take, if you will, agriculture first. Without the smith's art from which it borrows spade, ploughshare, sickle, axe, and other things beside; without that of the carpenter, so as both to frame a plough and to prepare a yoke and a cart to bruise the ears; and without the builder's to build a stable for the bullocks that plough, and the houses for the farmer that sows; and without the woodman's, to cut wood; and without the baker's after all these, agriculture is nowhere to be found. So the art of the weaving, when it produces anything, calls for many arts, together with itself to assist it in the works set before it; and if they are not present and stretch forth the hand, this too stands, like the former, at a loss. Indeed every one of the arts stands in need of the other.

But when alms are to be given, we need nothing else; only the disposition is required. If you say that money is needed, and houses and clothes and shoes, then read those words of Christ, which he spoke concerning the widow [Mk 12:43], and cease from this anxiety. However poor you are and even if you are poorer than the one who begs, cast in two mites and you will have fulfilled everything. Even when you have but a barley cake, and that is all you have, give it and you will have achieved the summit of this art. . . .

66.3. . . . Let us consider these things then, my beloved, and let us discern the truth at length, though late, and let us grow sober. I am now ashamed of speaking almsgiving, because, though I have often spoken on this subject, I have achieved nothing worthy of the exhortation. There has indeed been some increase, but not as much as I wished. I see you sowing, but not with a liberal hand. I therefore fear lest you also reap sparingly [2 Cor 9:6].

As proof that we do sow sparingly, let us inquire, if you please, who are more numerous in the city, poor or rich; and who, neither poor nor rich, are the middle group. As for instance, a tenth part is rich, and a tenth is poor that has nothing at all, and the rest is the middle group. Let us distribute then among the poor the whole multitude of the city, and you will see how great is our disgrace. The very rich are indeed but few, but those who come next to them are many; again, the poor are much fewer than these. Nevertheless, although there are so many that are able to feed the hungry, many go to sleep in their hunger, not because those that have are not able with ease to succor them, but because of their great barbarity and inhumanity. For if both the wealthy and those next to them were to distribute among themselves those who are in need of bread and clothing, one poor person would scarcely fall to the share of fifty people or even a hundred. Yet, they are waiting every day, despite the fact there is a great abundance of those who can help them.

And that you may learn the inhumanity of the others, consider how the church, whose revenue is one of the lowest among the wealthy, and not of the very rich, has assisted every numberless widows and virgins; indeed the list of them has already reached the number of three thousand. Together with these she assists those who are in prison, those who suffer in hospitals, those who are in convalescence, those who are away from home, those who are maimed, those who wait upon the altar; and with respect to food and clothing, those who happen to come every day. Her substance is in no respect diminished. If ten people alone were thus willing to spend, there would be no poor.

4. And what, it will be said, are our children to inherit? The principal remains, the income again has become more abundant, and the goods are being stored up for them in heaven. But are you not willing to do this? At least do it by the half, at least by the third part, at least by the fourth part, at least by the tenth. Owing to God's favor, it would be possible for our city to nourish the poor of ten cities. . . . What kind of defense will we have for not even out of our income giving to the hungry and distressed? . . .

I am not constraining you to lessen your capital, not because I do not wish it, but because I see you are very defiant and stubborn. . . . But give away the revenues, keep nothing of these. It is enough for you to have the money of your income pouring in on you as from a fountain; make the poor sharers with you, and become a good steward of the things God has given you. . . .

77.3. . . . This parable [of the faithful servant, Matt 24:45–47] applies to not only money only but also to speech, power, gifts, and every stewardship with which each is entrusted. It would suit rulers in the state also because everyone is bound to make full use of what one has for the common good. If it is wisdom that you have, or power, or wealth, or whatever, let it not be for the ruin of your fellow servants nor for your own ruin. . . .

Let us who have money listen to these things as well. Christ speaks not only to teachers but also to the rich. Both have been entrusted with riches: the teachers with the more necessary wealth, the rich with the inferior one. While the teachers are giving out the greater wealth, you are not willing to show forth your generosity even in the lesser, or rather not generosity but honesty (for you are in fact giving things that belong to others), what excuse will you have? . . .

4. You too are stewards of your own possessions, not less than he[2] who dispenses the alms of the church. Just as he has no right to squander at random and at hazard the things given by you for the poor, since they were given for the maintenance of the poor, so you may not squander your own. Even though you have received an inheritance from your father and have in this way come to possess everything you have, still everything belongs to God. Even as you for your part desire that what you have given should be thus carefully dispensed, do you not think that God will require his own of us with greater strictness, or that he allows them to be wasted at random? Certainly not. Because for this end, he left these things in your hand, in order to "give them their meat in due season." But what does it mean, "in due season?" To the needy, to the hungry. As you gave to your fellow servant to dispense, even so wills the Lord you to spend these things on what is needful.

Therefore, though he could have taken these possessions away from you, God left them so that you may have the opportunity to show forth virtue. Thus, bringing us into need one of another, he makes our love for one another more fervent. . . .

6. . . . If in worldly matters no one lives for oneself, but artisan, soldier, farmer, and merchant, all of them contribute to the common good, and to their neighbor's advantage, we must do this much more in spiritual things—because this is the most proper way to live. One who lives for oneself alone and overlooks all others is useless; that person is not even a human being and does not belong to the human race.

2. Clergy, i.e., priest or deacon under the direction of a bishop.

Homilies on the Acts of the Apostles

20.4. . . . . Nothing is more frigid than a Christian who does not care for the salvation of others. You cannot plead poverty here; for she who cast in her two mites will be your accuser [Luke 21:1]. Peter said: "Silver and gold I have none" [Acts 3:6]. Paul was so poor that he was often hungry and lacked the necessary food. You cannot plead lowliness of birth; for they [the apostles] too were ignoble men of ignoble parents. You cannot allege lack of education: for they too were "unlearned men" [Acts 4:13]. Even if you are a slave therefore and a runaway slave, you can still do your part, as exemplified by Onesimus. . . . You cannot plead infirmity; for Timothy too often had infirmities.

Every one can profit one's neighbor, if people will fulfill their part. Do you not see the unfruitful trees, how strong they are, how beautiful, how large, and smooth, and tall? But if we had a garden, we surely should much rather have pomegranates or fruitful olive trees than those trees that are delightful to the eyes but have but little profit. Such are those who only consider their own interest, or rather, not even such, since these persons are only fit for burning, whereas those trees are at least useful for building houses and protecting those who live in them.

Do not say: "It is impossible for me to care for the others." If you are a Christian, it is impossible that it should be so. As the natural properties of things cannot be made ineffectual, so it is here: the thing is part of the very nature of the Christian. Do not insult God. To say that the sun cannot shine would be to insult him. To say that a Christian cannot do good is to insult God and call him a liar. It is easier for the sun not to give heat or not to shine than for the Christian not to spend forth light; it is easier for the light to be darkness than for the Christian to be so.

[handwritten margin note: caring is the very nature of being a Christian]

Homilies on the Letter to the Ephesians

21.2. . . . Let us consider everything as secondary to the provident care we should take of our children, and to our "bringing them up with the training and instruction befitting the Lord" [Eph 6:4]. If from the very beginning they are taught to be a lover of true wisdom, then they have acquired a wealth superior to all other wealth and a glory superior to all other glory. You will achieve nothing as great by teaching them an art, and giving them that worldly [i.e., classical] learning by which they will gain riches, as by teaching them the art of despising riches. If you desire to make them rich, do this. True—the rich are not those who desire many riches and are encircled with abundant wealth, but those who have need of nothing. Discipline your children in this; teach them this. This is the greatest riches. Do not seek how to give them reputation and high fame in worldly learning, but consider deeply how you will teach them to despise the glory that belongs to this present life. In this way they will become more distinguished and more truly glorious. This is possible the poor and the rich alike to accomplish. . . .

Wealth is harmful, because it renders us unprepared for the vicissitudes of life. Let us therefore bring up our children to be such that they will be able to bear up against every trial, and not be surprised at what may come upon them. . . . And great will be the reward that will thus be reserved for us. If people enjoy so great honor for making statues and painting portraits of kings, will we, who adorn the image of the King of kings (for humanity is the image of God), not receive ten thousand blessings if we produce a true likeness? The likeness resides in the virtue of the soul, when we train our children to be good, to be meek, to be forgiving (all these are attributes of God), to be beneficent, to be human, and when we train them to take little account of this world. Let this then be our task, to mold and direct both ourselves and them according to what is right.

Homilies on the First Letter to Timothy

 # wealth is a loan for use

11.2. . . . The wealth is not a possession; it is not property, it is a loan for use. For how can you claim that it is a possession if when you die, willingly or unwillingly, all that you have goes to others, and they again give it up to others, and these again to others. We are all sojourners; and the tenant of the house is perhaps more truly the owner of it, for when the owner dies, the tenant lives on and still enjoys the house; and if the tenant has to pay for enjoying the house, the owner too has to pay for it to have it built and has to endure thousands of pains to have it fitted up. Property, in fact, is but a word; we are all owners but of other people's possessions.

Only those things are our own which we have sent before us to the other world. Our goods here are not our own; we have only a life interest in them; or rather they fail us even here on earth. Only the virtues of the soul are properly our own, as almsgiving and charity. Worldly goods were called external things, even by those who are outside the church,[3] because they are external to us. But let us make them internal. We cannot take our wealth with us when we depart from here, but we can take our charities. Let us rather send them before us so that they may prepare for us an abode in the eternal mansions [Luke 16:9].

Riches [*chrēmata*] are named from use [*kechrēsthai*], not from ownership, and are not our own; and possessions are not a property but a loan. If not, then tell me through how many more hands it will pass. There is a well-known wise proverb (and popular proverbs, when they contain any wisdom, are not to be despised): "O field, how many people's have you been and how many more people's will you be?" This we should say to our houses and all our goods. Virtue alone is able to depart with us and to accompany us to the world above. Let us then give up and extinguish that love of wealth, that we may kindle in us a desire for eternal things. These two affections cannot possess one soul. For it is said, "Either one will hate the

---

3. For example, Stoic philosophers.

one, and love the other; or else one will hold to the one, and despise the other" [Matt 6:24].

12.3. . . . But you who are experienced in worldly affairs, do you not know how many people, after infinite toils, have not enjoyed the fruits of their labors, whether because they are prematurely cut off by death, or overtaken by misfortunes, or assailed by disease, or ruined by false accusers, or some other causes, which amidst the variety of human casualties, has forced them to go empty-handed?

But some will object to me: "Don't you see the lucky ones who with little labor acquire the good things of life?" But what good things? Money, houses, so many acres of land, trains of servants, heaps of gold and silver? Can you call these good things and not hide your head for shame? How can a person, called to the pursuit of heavenly wisdom, lust after worldly things, and name these valueless things "goods"? If these things are good, then their possessors must be called good. For is not the one good who is the possessor of what is good? But when the possessors of these things are guilty of fraud and robbery, shall we call them good? If wealth is a good but is increased by greed, the greedier one is, the better the possessor must be. But is not this plainly a self-contradiction? But suppose the wealth is not gained wrongfully. But how is this possible? So destructive a passion is greed, that to grow rich without injustice is impossible. Christ declared this, saying: "Make to yourselves friends of the mammon of unrighteousness" [Luke 16:9]. But what if, you say, a man succeeded to his father's inheritance? Then he received what had been gathered by injustice. For it was not from Adam that his ancestor inherited riches, but of the many who were before him, some one must probably have unjustly taken and enjoyed the goods of others. What then? He says, did Abraham hold unrighteous wealth; and Job, that blameless righteous, and faithful man, who "feared God and eschewed evil?" Theirs was a wealth that consisted not in gold and silver, nor in houses, but in cattle. Furthermore, he [Job] was enriched by God. And the author of that book, relating what happened to that blessed man, mentions the loss of his camels, his mares and asses, but does not speak of treasures of gold or silver being taken away. The riches of Abraham too were his domestics. What then? Did he not buy them? No, for to this very point the Scripture says that the three hundred and eighteen were born in his house [Gen 19:14]. He had also sheep and oxen. From where then did he send gold to Rebekah [Gen 12:16; 24:22]? From the gifts which he received from Egypt without violence or wrong.

4. Tell me, then, where do you get your riches from? From whom did you receive it and from whom did he receive who transmits it to you? "From my father and he from my grandfather." But can you, going back through many generations show that the riches were justly acquired? No, you cannot. The root and origin of them must have been injustice. Why? It is because God in the beginning made not one rich and another poor. Nor did he afterwards take a show to one treasures of gold, and deny the other the right of searching for it. Rather, he left the earth free to all alike. How come then, if it is common, you have acres and acres of land, while your neighbor has not a portion of it? "My father transmitted them to me," you say. But from whom did he receive them? "From my grandfather." But you must go back and find its original answer.

Jacob made himself rich, but he gained wealth as a reward for his just labors. However, I will not urge this argument too closely. Let us say that riches should be justly gained and without rapine. You are not responsible for the covetous acts of your father. Your wealth may be derived from rapine; but you did not commit the act of plunder, that his gold was dug up somewhere out of the earth. What then? Is wealth therefore good? By no means! "But it is not bad, either," you say. Yes, it is not bad or evil if you are not avaricious and distribute it to the poor. "But if I do not do evil, even though I do not do good, it is not bad," you retort. True. But is not this an evil, that you alone should have the Lord's property, that you alone should enjoy what is common? Is not "the earth God's, and the fullness thereof" [cf. Ps 24:1]? Thus if our possessions belong to one common Lord, they belong also to our fellow servants.

The possessions of the Lord are common. Do we not see this the established rule in great houses? To all is given an equal share of provisions, because they proceed from the treasures of the Lord. And the house of the master is open to all. The King's possessions are all common: cities, market places, and public walks. We all share them equally.

Observe the wise dispensation of God. To put humanity to shame he has made certain things in common, such as the sun, air, earth, water, heaven, sea, light, stars. Their benefits are dispensed equally to all as siblings. We are all formed with the same eyes, the same body, the same soul, the same structure in all respects, all things from the earth, all people from one human being, and all in the same habitation. But these are not enough to shame us. He has also made other things common, as we have said: baths, cities, market places, and walks.

Observe further now concerning things that are common; there is no contention, but everything is peaceful. But as soon as someone attempts to possess oneself of anything to make it one's own, then contention is introduced; it is as if nature itself protests against the fact that, whereas God brings us together in every way, we are eager to divide and separate ourselves by appropriating things, using those cold words "mine and yours." Then struggles and hatred arise. But where this does not happen, no strife or struggles appear.

Hence we should conclude that common sharing is more convenient and more agreeable to our nature. Why it is that there is never a dispute about a market place? Is it not because it is common to all? But about a house, about a property, about money, disputes never come to an end. Things that necessary are set in common, whereas in the least things, we do not observe community and equality. Yet God has opened freely to all those greater things so that we may learn to share in common these inferior things. Nevertheless, for all this, we have not learned the lesson.

But as I said, how can the rich be good? When they distribute their riches, they are good, so that they are good when they have ceased to have it, when they give it to others; but while they keep it themselves, they are not good. How then is that a good which being retained renders people evil, being parted with what makes them good? Not therefore to have wealth, but to have it not, makes one appear to be good. Wealth therefore is not a good. But if, when you can receive it, you do not receive it, again you are good. . . . According to this rule, the more charitable you are, the more good you will be considered. But if you are rich, you are no longer good. Let us therefore become good in this way that we may be really good and may obtain the good things to come in Jesus Christ.

11

Ambrose of Milan

On Naboth[1]

1. The story of Naboth,[2] ancient though it may be, has perennial application. Daily the rich and prosperous covet other people's goods, daily they endeavor to dispossess the humble, robbing the poor of their possession, their little ancestral plot of ground. Discontented with what they have, they feel their craving enkindled by any property of their neighbors. So that Ahab is not one person, someone born long ago; every day, alas, the world sees Ahabs born, never to die out—or if one such dies, a multitude rises up instead, and the spoilers still outnumber the spoiled. And Naboth is not one person either, a poor man who was once murdered; every day some Naboth is put to death, every day the poor are murdered. . . .

2. You rich, how far will you push your frenzied greed? Are

1. Based on the Latin texts I have revised and expanded Peter C. Phan's translation in *Social Thought* (Message of the Fathers of the Church 20; Wilmington, DE: Glazier, 1984). Used by permission.
2. See 1 Kings 21.

you alone to dwell on the earth? Why do you cast out people who are fellow creatures and claim all creation as your own? Earth at its beginning was for all in common, it was meant for rich and poor alike; what right do you have to monopolize the soil? Nature knows nothing of the rich; all are poor when she brings them forth. Clothing and gold and silver, food and drink and covering—we are born without them all; naked she receives her children into the tomb, and no one can enclose one's acres there. . . .

4. But in their lifetime even, why should they think they have everything in plenty? You, the rich who call yourselves rich, you do not know how needy you are, how truly impoverished you feel? The more you have, the more you want; and however much you win, you are still poor in your own eyes. Greed is not quenched by gain; it is fanned even more. . . . Holy Scripture shows us how wretchedly poor the rich may be, and how abject beggars they may be.

5. Ahab was king of Israel, Naboth a poor man. The one enjoyed a whole kingdom's affluence, the other possessed a little holding. Naboth coveted none of the rich man's estates; Ahab considered himself in need because his poor neighbor had a vineyard. Which of them do you think was poor? . . .

But let us look at the words of Scripture. "And some time after this, as Naboth the Jezraelite had a vineyard in Jezrael near the palace of Ahab, king of Samaria, Ahab said to Naboth; 'Give to me your vineyard, that I may make of it a garden of herbs, because it is near my house, and I will give you for it another vineyard; or if it seems good to you, I will give you money for the vineyard, and I will make of it a garden of herbs.' Naboth said to Ahab: 'God forbid that I should give you the inheritance of my fathers.' Ahab went home disturbed; he lay on his bed and covered his face and would not eat" [1 Kgs 21:1–4]. . . . What does the king have to say? Listen. "Give to me." Are these the words of the poor, of some beggar in the streets? "Give to me." Give to me—I am in want; give to me—I am without other means of livelihood; give to me—I have no means to eat or drink, to keep or to clothe myself, not a loaf, not a coin, nothing at all. Give to me—the Lord has given nothing. Give to me; I am helpless unless you give. Give to me; it is written, "give alms." How servile, how despicable all this is! There is no feeling of humility in it, only a burning greed. But what arrogance also in the servile words! Give me *your* vineyard, he says; he acknowledges that it is not his, that he has no claim to it, but he asks for it nonetheless. "And I will give you for it another vineyard." The rich man disdains as worthless what is his own, and covets as something most precious what is another's. "Or if it seems good to you, I will give you money." He quickly covers his first mistake, and offers money instead of another vineyard; his own properties are to reach out everywhere, and no one else should have property at all. . . .

11. "And I will make of it a garden of herbs." This was the aim, then, of all his wild frenzy; space was needed for common herbs. Such are you, rich; you are not so anxious to own for use—rather you wish to shut others out. You are more concerned to rob the poor than to gain anything for yourselves. You think it is an affront to you, if the poor has something the rich might care to own; and anything that belongs to others, you consider a loss to you. What pleasure can come to you from this waste of nature's wealth? The world was created for all in general, yet a handful of the rich endeavor to make it their own preserve. . . .

44. How vividly does the Scripture portray the rich and their ways! They are disconsolate if they cannot rob their neighbors, they refuse to eat, they fast—not to lessen their crime but to accomplish it. At such times you see them joining the congregation at church—dutiful, demure, regular—hoping to win the grace to effect their evil purpose. But God says to them: "This is not the fast that I have chosen, that you bow your head like a reed or be in sackcloth or ashes. You shall not call this an acceptable fast. . . . But loose every bond of wickedness, undo the knots of covenants made by force, let the afflicted go free, tear up very unjust writing. Give bread to the hungry; and bring the needy and homeless into your house" [Isa 58:5–7]. . . .

On Tobit

2.7. If I lend money without demanding interest, I act justly. Indeed, lending with the expectation of interest is unjust, but lending itself is not, as it is written: "Lend to your neighbor in his hour or need" [Sir 29:2]. David too has said: "The just man is kind and lends" [Ps 37:21]. But the other kind of lending, which is done in order to gain profit, is rightly condemned as abominable and is forbidden by the law [cf. Deut 23:19]. Tobit shuns taking interest: he instructs his son not to despise God's commandments, to give alms from his possessions, not to lend his money with interest, not to turn his face from any of the poor [cf. Tob 4:6–9]. Whoever gives this advice condemns interest-taking, which is for many the way to make a profit and occasion to do commerce. Buy usury is forbidden to the saints.

8. The more blameworthy usury is, the more admirable the one who abstains from it is. If you have money, give it away. The money that you keep idle, make it useful for others. Give it with the intention of not recovering it; and if it is returned to you, do not receive profit from it. If the borrower cannot pay your money back to you, let him repay you his gratitude; if you are cheated of your money, you will acquire justice, because one who has compassion and lends is just. If you lose your money, you will gain mercy, as it is written: "He is merciful who lends to his neighbor" [Sir 29:1]. . . .

11. You rich, such are indeed your favors! You give little and demand much in return. This is your compassion: you plunder even when you say you are giving help. For you even the poor are a source of profit. You subject the poor to usury; you know how to oblige them to pay you interest even when they do not have enough to look after their basic needs. Truly compassionate you are! You grant them freedom and then bind them to yourselves; you oblige them to pay you interest even when they have nothing to eat. Can one imagine anything more perverse? The poor ask for medicine and you offer them poison; they beg for bread and you give them a sword; they plead for freedom and you subject them to slavery; they implore to be

freed from their bonds and you entrap them in an inescapable net.

On the Duties of the Clergy[3]

1.11.38. Mercy, also, is a good thing because it makes people perfect insofar as it imitates the perfect Father. Nothing graces the Christian soul so much as mercy. It is exercised chiefly towards the poor; you should consider them as sharers with you in the common fruits of the earth, which brings them forth for the use of all. Consequently you should distribute to the poor what you have and in this way help your brothers and sisters and companions. You give money, the poor receive life; the money you give is their livelihood; your money makes up their prosperity.

39. Furthermore, the poor give more to you than you to them, since they are your debtor in regard to your salvation. If you clothe the naked, you clothe yourself with righteousness. If you welcome the stranger into your home and receive the needy, they will procure for you the friendship of the saints and an eternal dwelling-place [cf. Luke 16:9]. That is no small recompense. You sow earthly things and receive heavenly rewards. . . . Do you wonder at the judgment of God in the case of holy Job? Wonder rather at his virtue in that he could say: "I was an eye to the blind, and a foot to the lame. I was a father to the poor. Their shoulders were made warm with the skins of my lambs. The stranger dwelt not at my gates, but my door was open to every one that came" [Job 29:15–16]. Clearly blessed are those from whose house the poor have never gone with empty hands. Again, no one is more blessed than those who are sensible of the needs of the poor and the hardships of the weak and helpless. In the Day of Judgment they will receive salvation from the Lord, whom they will have as their debtor for the mercy they have shown [cf. Prov. 19:7]. . . .

1.28.130. Justice, then, concerns the society and the community of the human race. For what hold society together is

3. Translations of this text and the next are mine.

divided into two parts: justice and good-will. The latter is also called liberality and kindness. Of the two, justice seems to me the loftier, liberality the more pleasing. The one gives judgment, the other shows goodness.

131. But what the pagan philosophers take to be the first duty of justice is not acceptable to us. They maintain, in fact, that the first expression of justice is to hurt no one, unless one is provoked to do so by the wrongs received. This opinion is contradicted by the authority of the Gospel. The Scripture wills that we should imitate the spirit of the Son of man, who came to give grace, not to bring harm [Luke 9:56].

132. Next they considered it compatible with justice that one should treat common, that is, public property as public, and private as private. But this is not even in accord with nature, for nature has poured forth all things for all for common use. God has ordered all things to be produced, so that there should be food in common to all, and that the earth should be a kind of common possession for all. Nature, therefore, has produced a common right for all, but greed has made it a right for a few. Here, too, we are told that the Stoics taught that all things that the earth produces have been created for the human use, and that humanity has been born for the sake of humanity, so that one may be of mutual advantage to another.

133. But from where have they got such ideas except out of the holy Scriptures? For Moses wrote that God said: "Let us make humans in our image, after our likeness, and let them have dominion over the fish of the sea, and over the birds of the air, and over the cattle, and over every creeping thing that creeps upon the earth" [Gen 1:26]. . . . So these philosophers have learned from our writings that all things were made subject to humanity, and therefore, they think that all things were produced also for human sake. . . .

135. Thus, in accordance with the will of God and the bonds of nature, we must assist one another, vie with one another in doing good works, lay, as it were, all our advantages before all, and [to use the words of the Scripture] bring help to each other from a feeling of devotion or of duty, by giving money,

or by doing something, one way or another, so that among us the good of the society may be increased. Let no one shirk from these duties for fear of danger but let people consider all affairs of the society, whether good or evil, as their own concern. . . .

2.28.136. It is a great incentive to mercy to share in other people's misfortunes, to help them as far as our means allow, and sometimes even beyond them. It is better for mercy's sake to take up a case, or to suffer hatred rather than to show lack of feeling. I once brought hatred on myself because I broke up the sacred vessels to redeem captives—a fact that could displease the Arians. It was not the act itself that displeased them; rather it was a pretext they could use to blame me. Who indeed can be so hard, so cruel, and so cold-hearted as to be displeased by the fact a man is saved from death, or a woman from barbarian rapes, things that are worse than death, or boys and girls and infants from the pollution of idols, whereby through fear of death they were defiled?

137. Although we did not act in that way without good reason, we have pursued this matter with the people in order to confess and to proclaim again and again that it was far better to preserve souls than gold for the Lord. He who sent the apostles without gold, also founded the church without gold. The church possesses gold, not to store up, but to distribute and to use it to help those in want. What need is there to guard what is useless to anyone if it is kept? Do we not know how much gold and silver the Assyrians carried off from the Lord's temple? Is it not far better that the priests should melt it down to support the poor, if other supplies fail, than to have it plundered and defiled by a sacrilegious enemy? The Lord himself would say: "Why did you allow so many needy to die of hunger? Surely you do have gold. You should have given them food and sustenance. Why are so many captives brought to the slave market and why are so many unredeemed left to be killed by the enemy? It would be better to preserve living vessels than gold ones." . . .

3.4.25. It is clear, then, that we should consider and admit that what benefits the individual is the common good and should judge nothing as useful unless it benefits all. How can one be benefitted alone? What is useless to all is harmful. I certainly cannot conceive that what is useless to all can be of use to anyone at all. For if there is only one law of nature for all, there is also only one state of usefulness for all. And we are bound by the law of nature to act for the good of all. It is not, therefore, right for the person who wishes the interests of another to be considered according to nature, to injure that person against the law of nature.

Letter 2

To Bishop Constantius (before Lent 379)

2.11. Let your people not desire many things; a few things are already many to them. Poverty and riches are words which imply want and satiety. Those who do not have everything they desire are not rich, nor are they poor who have. Let no one despise a widow, or cheat on orphan, or defraud one's neighbor. Woe to those who have amassed a fortune by deceit and build a city in blood, that is, their souls, because it is the soul that is built like a city. Greed does not build it, but sets it on fire and burns it. Do you want to build your city well? "Better is a little with the fear of the Lord than great treasures without fear" [Prov 15:16]. People's riches should work towards the redemption of their souls, not to their destruction. Wealth is redemption if one uses it well; it is a snare if one does not know how to use it. For what is people's money if not provision for their journey? A great amount is a burden; a moderate sum is useful. We are pilgrims in this life; many are walking along, but we must make a good journey in order to have Christ as our fellow-traveler who spent his life on earth doing good. . . . A good name is more excellent than money, and above heaps of silver is good favor [cf. Prov 22:1]. Faith itself redounds to itself, sufficiently rich and more than rich in its possession. . . .

15. Happy are the ones who have been able to cut out the root of vices, avarice. Surely they will not fear the balance

of justice. Avarice generally dulls people's senses and pervert judgments, so that they think profit as piety and money as reward of prudence. But great is the reward of piety and the advantage of moderation; the possession of these virtues is sufficient. For, what do superfluous riches profit in this world if they do not assist our birth and impede our dying? Naked we are born into this world, we leave it in destitution, and we are buried without our inheritance. . . . Urge the people of the Lord to hope more in the Lord, therefore, to abound in the riches of simplicity, in which they may walk without a snare, without hindrance. . . .

16. Let your people seek the riches of good works and be rich in character. The beauty of riches is not in the purses of the rich, but in their support of the poor. In the weak and needy, riches shine brighter. Let the wealthy learn to seek not their own interests, but those of Christ's, so that Christ may seek them out and bestow his possessions on them. He spent his blood for them; he poured his spirit; he offers them his kingdom. What else can he give who has given himself? Or what will the Father refuse to give, who delivered his only begotten Son to death for us? Therefore, admonish them to serve the Lord in purity and grace, to lift up their eyes to heavenly things with all the intensity of their minds, to count nothing as gain except what profits eternal life, since all the gain of this world is the loss of souls. Finally, the one who wished to gain Christ suffered the loss of all things, . . . but Christ has said: "If any want to come after me let them deny themselves" [Luke 9:23]. In this way they become their own loss, that they may become Christ's gain. All such possessions are perishable, accompanied by loss and without gain. There is gain only where there is everlasting enjoyment, where eternal peace is the reward.

12

Augustine of Hippo

On Christian Doctrine[1]

1.3.3. There are some things which are to be enjoyed, others which are to be used, and others which are enjoyed and used. Those that are to be enjoyed make us happy. Those that are to be used help us as we strive for happiness and, in a certain sense, sustain us so that we are able to arrive at and cling to those things that make us happy. But, if we who enjoy and use things, living as we do in the midst of both kinds of things, strive to enjoy the things which we are supposed to use, we find our progress impeded and even now and then turned aside. As a result, fettered by love for lesser goods, we are either delayed in gaining those things that we are to enjoy or we are even drawn away entirely from them.

4. To enjoy anything means to cling to it with affection for its own sake. To use a thing is to employ what we have received

1. Based on the Latin texts I have revised and expanded Peter C. Phan's translation in *Social Thought* (Message of the Fathers of the Church 20; Wilmington, DE: Glazier, 1984). Used by permission.

for our use to obtain what we desire, provided that it is a proper object of our desire. A bad use should rather be called an abuse. Suppose, then, we were travelers in a foreign land, who could not live in contentment except in our own native country; if, unhappy because of that traveling abroad and wishing to end our misery, we planned to return home, it would be necessary to use some means of transportation, either by land or sea, to enable us to reach the land we were to enjoy. But, if the pleasantness of the journey and the very movement of the vehicles were to delight us and turn us aside to enjoy the things which we should merely use instead, and were to confuse us by false pleasure, we would be unwilling to end our journey quickly and would be alienated from the land whose pleasantness would make us really happy. Just so, wanderers from God on the road of this mortal life, if we wish to return to our native country where we can be happy, we must use this world, and not enjoy it, so that the "invisible attributes" of God may be clearly seen, "being understood through the things that are made" [Rom 1:20], that is, that through what is material and temporal we may comprehend the eternal and spiritual.

Letters

130: To Proba[2] (c. 412)

3. Through love of this true life you must, then, consider yourself desolate in this world, no matter what happiness you enjoy. Just as that is the true life in comparison with which this other life (which is so much loved) is not worthy to be called life, however pleasant and prolonged it may be, so that is the true comfort which God promised by the prophet [Isaiah] saying: "I will give them true comfort, peace upon peace" [Isa

---

2. A noble Roman widow, whose husband was Probus, praetorian prefect and one-time consul. She, with her daughter-in-law Juliana and granddaughter Demetrias the virgin, fled to North Africa in the aftermath of the sack of Rome by the Visigoths (410). Augustine refers to them in his treatise on *Widowhood* and Jerome praises Proba in his letter to Demetrias (*Letter* 8). Pelagius also wrote a letter to Demetrias.

57:18–19]. Without this comfort there is more grief than consolation to be found in earthly comforts, whatever they may be. Certainly, as far as riches and high-ranking positions and other things of that sort are concerned—things which people think themselves happy to possess because they have never partaken of that true happiness—what comfort can they bestow, when it is a far better thing not to need them than to excel in them; and when we are tortured by the craving to possess them, but still more by the fear of losing, once we do possess them? People become good not by having such goods, but having become good otherwise, they make these things good by their good use of them. Therefore, there is no true comfort in these things; rather, it is found where true life is. One's happiness must necessarily come from the same source as one's goodness. . . .

12. Is it agreed, then, that over and above that temporal welfare people might wish for positions of rank and authority for themselves and their families? Certainly, it is proper for them to wish for these things, not for the sake of the things themselves, but for another reason, namely, that they might do good by providing for the welfare of those who live under them. But it is not proper to covet them out of the empty pride of self-esteem, or useless ostentation, or hurtful vanity. Therefore, if they wish for themselves and their families only what is sufficient of the necessities of life, as the Apostle says: "But godliness with contentment is a great gain. For we brought nothing into this world, and we can carry nothing out; but having food and clothing to be covered, with these we are content. Those who will become rich fall into temptation, and the snares of the devil and into many unprofitable and hurtful desires, which drown people into destruction and perdition. For the desire of money is the root of all evils, which some coveting have erred from the faith and have entangled themselves in many sorrows" [1 Tim 6:6–10]—this sufficiency is not an improper desire in whoever wishes this and nothing more; whoever does wish more does not wish this, and therefore does not wish properly. He wished this and prayed for it who said: "Give me not riches [or] poverty; give me only enough of the necessaries of

life, lest being filled I should become a liar and say: 'Who sees me'? or become poor, I should steal and denounce the name of my God" [Prov 30:8–9]. Surely you see that this sufficiency is not to be coveted for its own sake, but to provide for health of body and for clothing which accords with one's personal dignity, and which makes it possible for him or her to live with others honorably and respectably.

13. Among all these objects, one's personal safety and friendship are desired for their own sake, whereas a sufficiency of the necessities of life is usually sought—when it is properly sought—for the two reasons mentioned above, but not for its own sake. Now, personal safety is closely connected with life itself, health, and integrity of mind and body. In like manner, friendship is not confined by narrow limits; it includes all those to whom love and affection are due although it goes out more readily to some, more slowly to others; but it reaches even our enemies, for whom we are commanded to pray. Thus there is no one in the human race to whom love is not due, either as a return of mutual affection or in virtue of one's share in our common nature. But those who love us mutually in holiness and chastity give us the truest joy. These are the good we must pray to keep when we have them, to acquire when we do not have them. . . .

23. It is our duty to ask these things[3] without hesitation for ourselves, our friends, and for strangers—yes, even for enemies; although in the heart of the person praying, desire for one and for another may arise, differing in nature or in strength according to the more immediate or more remote relationship. But those who say in prayer such words as, "O Lord, multiply my riches"; or "Give me as much wealth as you have given to this or that one"; or "Increase my honors, make me eminent for power and fame in this world," or something else of this sort; and those who ask merely from a desire for these things, not in order to benefit others through them agreeably to God's will, I do not think that they will find any part of the Lord's Prayer in relation to which they could fit

3. They refer to the petitions in the Lord's Prayer.

in these requests. Therefore, let us be ashamed at least to ask these things, if we are not ashamed to desire them. However, if we are ashamed of even desiring them but feel ourselves overcome by the desire, how much better for us to ask him, to whom we say, "Deliver us from evil!" to free us from this plague of desire?

153: To Macedonius (c. 414)

26. Now, if we look carefully at what is written: "The whole world is the wealth of the faithful one, but the unfaithful one does not have a penny" [Prov 17:6 LXX], do we not prove that those who seem to rejoice in lawfully acquired gains but do not know how to use them, are really in possession of other people's property? Certainly, what is lawfully possessed is not another's property, but "lawfully" means justly, and justly means rightly. Those who use their wealth badly possess it wrongfully, and wrongful possession means that it is another's property. You see then how many there are who should make restitution of another's goods, although those to whom restitution is due may be few; wherever they are, their claim to just possession is the proportion to their indifference to wealth. Obviously, no one possesses justice unlawfully: whoever does not love it does not have it; but money is wrongly possessed by bad people while good people who love it least have the most right to it. In this life the wrong of evil possessors is endured and among them certain laws are established, which are called civil laws, not because they bring people to make a good use of their wealth, but because those who make a bad use of it become thereby less harmful to others. This comes about either because some of them become faithful and fervent—and these have a right to all things—or because those who live among them are not hampered by their evil deeds but are tested until they come to that City where they are heirs to eternity, where the just alone have a place, the wise alone leadership; and those who are there possess what is truly their own. Yet, even here, we do not intercede to prevent restitu-

tion from being made according to earthly customs and laws, although we should like you to be merciful to evil-doers, not to make them take pleasure or persist in their evil, but because, whenever any of them become good, God is appeased by the sacrifice of mercy; and if evil-doers did not find him merciful, there would be no good people.

157: To Hilarius[4] (414)

23. Now, listen to something about riches in answer to the next inquiry in your letter.[5] In it you wrote that some[6] are saying that a rich man who continues to live rich cannot enter the kingdom of heaven unless he sells all he has, and that it cannot do him any good to keep the commandments while he keeps his riches [cf. Matt 19:21–24; Mark 10:21–25; Luke 18:22–25]. Their arguments have overlooked our fathers, Abraham, Isaac, and Jacob, who departed from this life long ago. It is a fact that all these had extensive riches, as the Scripture faithfully bears witness. Yet Christ who became poor for our sakes [cf. 2 Cor 8:9], although he was truly rich, foretold in a truthful promise that many would come from the east and the west and would sit down not above them, or without them, but with them in the kingdom of heaven [cf. Matt 8:11]. Although the haughty rich man, who was clothed in purple and fine linen and feasted sumptuously every day, died and was tormented in hell, but if he had shown mercy to the poor man [Lazarus] covered with sores who lay at his door and was treated with scorn, he himself would have deserved mercy [Luke 16:19–31]. And if the poor man's merit had simply been his poverty, not his goodness, he surely would have not been carried by angels into the bosom of Abraham who had been rich in this life. This is intended to show us that on the one hand it was not poverty in itself that was divinely honored, nor, on the other, was it

---

4. A Sicilian layman, not to be identified with his namesakes, the bishop of Narbonne and a layman of Arles, both addressed by Augustine in his other letters.
5. Augustine, *Letter* 156.
6. Pelagius's followers had a more ascetic and radical view of wealth, making renunciation normative for all Christians, as exemplified in *On Riches* (*De divitiis*).

that riches were condemned, but that the godliness of the one and the ungodliness of the other had their own consequences; and, as the torment of fire was the lot of the ungodly rich man, so the bosom of the rich Abraham received the godly poor man. Although Abraham lived as a rich man, he held his riches so lightly and thought them of so little worth in comparison to God's commandments that he would not offend God by refusing to sacrifice, at his command, the very son whom he had hoped and prayed for as the heir of his riches [cf. Gen 22:1–10].

24. At this point they probably say that the patriarchs of old did not sell all they had and give to the poor, because the Lord had not commanded it. The New Testament had not yet been revealed; as it was fitting that it should not be until the fullness of time had come, so neither was it fitting that their virtue should be revealed. Yet God knew that they could easily exercise this virtue internally, and he bore such striking witness to them that, although he is the God of all the saints and of all righteous people, he deigned to speak of them as his particular friends: "I am the God of Abraham, and the God of Isaac and the God of Jacob; this is my name forever" [Exod 3:15]. But, after "the great mystery of godliness was manifested in the flesh" [1 Tim 3:16], and the coming of Christ was made visible by the calling of all nations—and the patriarchs, too, had believed in him but had preserved the faith, so to speak, in the root of the olive tree, of which the fruit was to be manifested in its own time, as the Apostle says [cf. Rom 11:17]—then, the rich man was told: "Sell all that you have, and give to the poor, and you will have treasure in heaven; and come, follow me" [Matt 19:21; Mark 10:21; Luke 18:22].

25. If they say this, they seem to speak with reason. But they should hear and take account of the whole, not open their ears to half of it and close them to the other half. To whom did the Lord give this commandment? Why to the rich man who was asking his advice on how to receive eternal life, for he had said to the Lord: "What shall I do that I may receive life everlasting" [Matt 19:16–22; cf. Mark 10:17–22; Luke 18:18–23]? He did not answer him: "If you wish to enter into life, sell all that you

have," but: "If you wish to enter into life, keep the commandments." And when the young man said that he had kept the commandments which the Lord had quoted to him from the law, and asked what was still lacking to him, he received this answer: "If you wish to be perfect,[7] go, sell all that you have and give to the poor." Lest he might think he was losing what he so dearly loved, the Lord said: "And you shall have treasure in heaven." Then he added: "And come, follow me" that no people who might do this should think it would bring them any reward unless they followed Christ. But the young man went away sad, so anyone can see how he kept those commandments of the law; I think he spoke with more pride than truth when he answered that he had kept them. However, it is a fact that the good Master distinguished between commandments of the law and that of higher perfection; for in the one place he said: "If you wish to enter into life, keep the commandments," but in the other: "If you wish to be perfect, sell all you have," and the rest. Why, then, do we refuse to admit that the rich, although far from that perfection, nonetheless enter into life if they keep the commandments, and give that it may be given to them, forgive that they may be forgiven [Luke 6:37–38]?

26. We believe that the apostle Paul was the minister of the New Testament when he wrote to Timothy, saying: "Tell the rich of this world not to be proud, not to trust in so uncertain a thing as wealth. Let them trust in the living God who gives us abundantly all things to enjoy. To do good, to be rich in good works, to give easily, to communicate to others, to lay up in store for themselves a good foundation against the time to come, that they may lay hold on the true life" [1 Tim 6:17–19]. In the same way, it was said to the young man: "If you wish to enter into life." I think that when he gave those instructions to the rich, the Apostle was not wrong in not saying: "Tell the rich of this world to sell all they have, give to the poor and follow the Lord," instead of: "Not to be proud, not to trust in so uncertain a thing as wealth." It was his pride, not his riches, that brought the rich man to the torments of hell, because he

---

7. This is again the Matthean version, which is favored by the church fathers.

despised the good poor man who lay at his gate, because he put his hope in uncertain riches, and thought himself happy in his purple and fine linen and sumptuous banquets [cf. Luke 16:19–20].[8]

27. But, perhaps, because the Lord continued and said: "Truly I say to you that a rich man will hardly enter into the kingdom of heaven. Again I say to you. It is easier for a camel to pass through the eye of a needle than for a rich man to enter into the kingdom of heaven," they think that, even if a rich man does the things which the Apostle prescribed for the rich, he cannot enter into the kingdom of heaven? What is the answer? Does the Apostle contradict the Lord, or do they not know what they say? Let the Christians choose which they will believe; I think it is better for us to believe that they do not know what they say than that Paul contradicts the Lord. Again, why do they not listen to the subsequent words of the Lord himself to his disciples, who were cast down at the wretched state of the rich: "What is impossible for mortals is easy for God"?

28. But, they say, this was said because it was going to happen that, hearing the Gospel, the rich would sell their inheritance, distribute to the poor, follow the Lord, and so enter into the kingdom of heaven; what seemed difficult would thus come to pass. According to them, it did not mean that those who retained their riches, even though they kept the Apostle's precepts of not being proud, trusting not in the uncertainty of riches but in the living God, of doing good, giving easily, and communicating to the needy, would thus lay hold on the true life, unless they carried out these apostolic directions by selling all their goods.

29. If they say this—and I know they do say it—they do not notice, in the first place, how the Lord preached his grace, con-

---

8. Note, as witnessed in other early Christian writers, how Augustine interprets one passage of the Scripture with another passage, conflating the rich man of Matthew 19 and also of Luke 16 into one composite figure, and harmonizing the commandments of Matthew 19 and 1 Timothy 6. He thus embraces and speaks for the "two-tiered" Christians with regard to wealth—the ascetics following the counsel of perfection and the ordinary Christians struggle along the way—and defends the "righteous rich" through almsgiving against the Pelagian critics of wealth.

trary to their teaching. He did not say: "What seems impossible for mortals is easy for them if they will it"; but he said: "What is impossible for mortals is easy for God," showing that when those actions are rightly performed, they are not done by the human power but by God's grace. Let them, then, take note of this, and, if they find fault with those who glory in their riches, let them take care themselves not to trust in their own strength, for both are rebuked in the Psalm: "Those who trust in their own strength and glory in the multitude of their riches" [Ps 49:6 (48:7 LXX)]. Let the rich listen to this: "What is impossible for mortals is easy for God." Whether they retain riches and do their good works by using them, or enter into the kingdom of heaven by selling them and distributing them to provide for the needs of the poor, let them attribute their good works to the grace of God, not to their own strength. What is impossible for mortals is easy, not for them, but for God. Let your friends hear that, and, if they have already sold all their goods and distributed them to the poor, or are still making plans and arrangements to do so and in this way are preparing to enter into the kingdom of heaven, let them not attribute this to their own strength, but to the same divine grace. For what is impossible for mortals is easy, not for them because they are mortals, but for God. The Apostle also says this to them: "With fear and trembling, work out your salvation. For it is God who works in you both to will and to accomplish, according to his good will" [Phil 2:12–13]. True, they say that by selling their goods they have followed the Lord's counsel of perfection, since it is added: "And come, follow me." Why, then, in the good works which they do, do they rely entirely on their own will and fail to hear the reproach and testimony of the Lord, whom they say they are following: "Without me, you can do nothing" [John 15:5]?

30. The Apostle said: "Tell the rich of this world not to be proud, not to trust in so uncertain a thing as wealth." If he meant that they should sell all they had and gain their reward by distributing it to the needy, then how do you make sense of what follows: "to give easily, to communicate to others, to lay

up in store for themselves a good foundation against the time to come"? If he believed that otherwise they could not enter into the kingdom of heaven, he was deceiving those whose homes he so carefully set in order, warning and instructing how wives should behave to their husbands and husbands to wives, children to parents, parents to children, servants to masters, masters to servants;[9] for how could any of this be done without a home and family possessions?

33. It is clear that this obligation and state of life (i.e., giving up riches for Christ's sake rather than Christ for the sake of riches) include surely those who have received the counsel of perfection[10] with such excellent dispositions that they have sold their goods and distributed them to the poor, and, with their shoulders freed of every worldly burden that they bear the light yoke of Christ [cf. Matt 11:30]. But they also include the weaker souls, less capable of the glorious perfection, who nevertheless remember that they are Christians when they hear that they must give up Christ or lose all their possessions. They will rather lay hold on the "tower of strength against the face of the enemy" [Ps 61:3 (60:4 LXX)]. When they were building it by their faith, they reckoned the cost with which it could be completed [Luke 14:28], that is, they embraced the faith with the intention of renouncing this world not in word alone. For if they bought something, they were as ones not possessing it, and, if they used this world, they were as ones not using it [cf. 1 Cor: 7:30–31], placing their hope not in the uncertainty of riches, but in the living God [1 Tim 6:17].

34. Everyone who renounces this world renounces, without question, everything in it so that they may be Christ's disciples. When he had pronounced the parable of the cost necessary for building a tower, and of the preparation for war of one king against another, he added: "Whoever does not renounce all that one possesses cannot be my disciple" [Luke 16:33]. One renounces his riches, if he has any, either by not loving them and distributing them to the needy, thereby to be lightened

9. The "Household Codes" in Eph 5:21–6:19; Col 3:18–4:1; cf. 1 Pet 3:1–7.
10. Those who live an ascetic or monastic lifestyle. Cf. par. 39.

of useless burdens; or he does that by loving Christ more and transferring his hope from those riches to him, so using them as to give easily, to share, to lay up treasure in heaven, and to be ready to give them up as he would his parents and children and wife—if he were faced with the alternative of not having them unless he gave up Christ. If people renounce the world on any other terms when they draw near to the sacrament of faith (baptism), they do what blessed Cyprian mourned over in the case of the lapsed, saying: "They renounce the world in word only, not in deed" [Cyprian, *Letter* 11.1]. Surely it is to such ones, who in the wake of temptation are more afraid of losing their wealth than of denying Christ, that these words apply: "Here is the one who began to build and was not able to finish" [Luke 14:30]. They are also the ones who, while their adversary is yet afar off, send an embassy desiring peace, that is, at the approach and threat of temptation, before it hurts them, they agree to give up Christ and deny him rather than be deprived of what is dearer to them. And there are many such who even think that the Christian religion should help them to increase their riches and multiply earthly delights!

35. But this kind of people does not include the rich Christians who, although they possess riches, are not possessed by them; because they have renounced the world in truth and in their heart, they put no hope in such possessions. These use a sound discipline in training their wives, their children, and their whole household to cling to the Christian religion. Their homes, overflowing with hospitality, "receive the just person in the name of a just person that they may receive the reward of a just person" [Matt 10:41]. They give their bread to the hungry; they clothe the naked [cf. Isa 58:7; Matt 25:35–36]; they ransom the captive, "to lay up in store for themselves a good foundation for the time to come that they may lay hold on the true life" [1 Tim 6:19]. If it happens that they have to suffer the loss of their money for the faith of Christ, they hate their riches; if this world threatens them with bereavement or separation from their families, they hate their parents, siblings, children, wives; finally, if there is question of an agreement

with their adversary about the very life of their body, they go so far as to hate their own life, rather than risk being forsaken by a forsaken Christ. Why? Because on all these points they have received a commandment that they cannot otherwise be Christ's disciples.

36. But this commandment that they must hate even their own life for the sake of Christ does not mean that they own it as something that can be sold, or that they can lay hands on themselves and destroy it, but that they are ready to lose it by dying for the name of Christ rather than live a dying life by denying Christ. In the same way, the riches which they were not ready to sell at the summons of Christ, they must be ready to lose for Christ, lest by losing Christ they lose themselves with their riches. We have striking examples of this in the wealthy of both sexes raised on high by the glory of martyrdom. Thus, many who had previously shrunk from the perfection to be attained by selling their goods were suddenly made perfect by imitating the Passion of Christ; and those who clung to their riches through the frailty of flesh and blood, when suddenly faced with sin, have resisted for the faith even unto blood. There are others who have not won the crown of martyrdom, who have not taken to heart the high and noble counsel of perfection by selling their goods, yet they are free of deeds deserving damnation. They have fed Christ hungry, given drink to him thirsty, clothed him naked [cf. Matt 25:34–46], received him a wanderer, and, although they will not sit with Christ on a throne when he comes to judge, they will stand at the his right to receive the judgment of mercy: "Blessed are the merciful for they will obtain mercy" [Matt 5:7], and "judgment without mercy to those who have not done mercy, but mercy exalts itself above judgment" [Jas 2:13].

37. From now on, let those objectors cease to speak against the Scriptures; let them, in their sermons, encourage people to higher things without condemning lower ones. They are unable to preach holy virginity in their exhortations without condemning the marriage bond, although the Apostle teaches that "everyone has one's proper gift from God, one after this

manner, another after that" [1 Cor 7:7]. Let them then walk in the path of perfection by selling all their goods and spending them on works of mercy. However, if they are truly the poor of Christ, and if they store up, not for themselves but for Christ, why should they pronounce punishment on their weaker members before they have attained to the seats of Judgment? If they are the kind of people to whom the Lord says: "You shall sit on twelve seats, judging the twelve tribes of Israel" [Matt 19:28; Luke 22:30], and of whom the Apostle says: "Do you not know that we shall judge angels?" [1 Cor 6:3], let them rather make ready to receive into everlasting mansions, not the accursed but the charitable rich who have made friends of them through the mammon of iniquity (cf. Luke 16:9]. I think that some of those who babble these ideas without restraint or reason are supported in their needs by rich and religious Christians. We may say that the church has its own soldiers and its own provincial officers, of whom the Apostle says: "Who serves as a soldier at any time at his own charges?" It has its vineyard and its planters, its flock and its shepherds, of whom the Apostle goes on to say: "Who plants a vineyard and does not eat of its fruit? Who feeds a flock and does not drink of the milk of the flock?" [1 Cor 9:7]. Yet to offer such arguments as they offer would not be to plant a vineyard but to uproot it; it would not be to gather the flock for the pasture but to drive the sheep from the flock to destruction.

38. As those who are fed and clothed at the expense of the generous rich (for they accept nothing for their own necessities except from those who sell their goods) are not judged and condemned by the more perfect members of Christ who furnish their own needs with their own hands (a higher virtue which the Apostle strongly commends [cf. Acts 20:34; 1 Thess 4:11]), so they in turn should not condemn as Christians of lower grade those from whose resources they are supplied. But by right living and right teaching they rather should say to them: "If we have sown unto you spiritual things, is it a great matter if we reap your temporal things?" [1 Cor 9:11]. The servants of God who live by selling the honest works of their own

hands could, with much less impropriety, condemn those from whom they receive nothing, than could those others who are unable to work with their hands because of some bodily weakness, yet who condemn the very ones at whose expense they live.

Tractates on the Gospel of John

6.25. Failing everywhere else, what do they [the Donatists[11]] now allege against us, not knowing what to say? They have taken away our houses, they have taken away our estates. They bring forward wills. "See, Gaius Seius made a grant of an estate to the church over which Faustinus presided." Of what church was Faustinus bishop? What is the church? To the church over which Faustinus presided, said he. But Faustinus presided not over a church, but over a sect [the Donatists]. The dove, however, is the church. Why do you protest? We have not devoured houses; let the dove have them. Let us inquire who the dove is, and let her have them. You know, my beloved, that those houses of theirs are not Augustine's. And if you do not know it and think that I take pleasure in possessing them, God knows that I think of them [the Donatists] and what I suffer on their account. He knows my groaning, since he has deigned to impart to me something of the dove.

Behold, there are these estates. By what right do you assert your claim to them? By divine right or by human right? Let them answer: Divine right we have in the Scriptures, human right in the laws of kings. By what right does every person possess one's property? Is it not by human right? For by divine right: "The earth is the Lord's and the fullness thereof" [Ps 24:1]. The poor and the rich God made of one clay; the same earth supports alike the poor and the rich. By human right, however, one says: "This estate is mine, this house is mine, this servant is mine." By human right, however, is by right of the emperors. Why so? Because God has distributed humanity

---

11. A North African schismatic group that separated itself from the Church Catholic (Universal) during the Great Persecution (311 CE).

these very human rights through the emperors and kings of this world.

Do you wish us to read the laws of the emperors and to act by the estates according to these laws? If you found your possession on human right, let us recite the laws of the emperor; let us see whether they would allow the heretics to possess anything. But you say: "What is the emperor to me?" It is by his right that you possess the land. Take away rights created by emperors, then who will dare say: "That estate is mine, or that slave is mind, or this house is mine?" If, however, people possess these goods because they have received rights from the emperors, do you want us to read the laws, so that you may be glad that you possess even a single garden, and attribute it to nothing but the clemency of the dove that you are permitted to remain in possession even there? There are indeed laws well known to all in which the emperors have directed that those who, being outside the communion of the Catholic Church,[12] usurp to themselves the name of Christians and are not willing in peace to worship the Author of peace, may not dare to possess anything in the name of the church.

26. But you reply: "What do we have to do with the emperor?" We have already said that we are treating of human right. Now the Apostle would have us obey kings and honor them, saying: "Honor the king" [1 Pet 2:17]. Do not say then: "What do I have to do with the king?," since in that case what do you have to do with the possession? It is by rights derived from kings that possessions are enjoyed. You have said: "What do I have to do with kings?" Do not say then that the possessions are yours, since it is to those same rights, by which people enjoy their possessions, that you have referred them.

Do you claim to found your possessions of divine right? Well, then, let us consult the Gospel; let us see how far extends the Catholic Church of Christ, upon whom the dove came and said: "This is he who baptizes." In what ways, then, can one possess by divine right, who says, "I baptize" [the Donatists]; while the dove says, "This is he who baptizes"; and while the Scripture

12. Again, it is the church universal.

says: "My dove is one, the only one of her mother" [Song 6:9]? Why have you torn the dove? Rather, why have you torn your own bowels? While you are torn to pieces, the dove continues whole in entirety. Therefore, my beloved, if, every argument of theirs being refuted, they have nothing further to say, I will tell them what to do: Let them come to the Catholic Church, and together with us, they will have not only the earth, but also him who made heaven and earth.

Exposition on Psalm 38[13]

On Ps 38:7 (LXX; elsewhere 39:6)

11. . . . "He lays up treasure, and does not know for whom he gathers it" [Ps 38:7 (LXX; elsewhere 39:6)]. Folly and vanity! "Blessed is the one whose hope is the Lord, who has not respected vanities or lying deceits" [Ps 40:4 (39:5 LXX)]. "Wild talk," you think (I speak to the very one who has a craving for treasure); "such words are nothing but old wives' tales." You are a careful, sensible person; every day you devise new means of making money—from business, from farming, perhaps from oratory and legal practice, perhaps from warfare; and there is usury besides. You are shrewd; you use every act you know to add coin to coin and to shroud your growing wealth in jealous secrecy. Robbing others, you are anxious not to be robbed yourself; you fear to suffer the wrong [you do to others], though your suffering does not atone for your sin. But, of course, with you there is no suffering; you are a cautious man, and as good at keeping money as at getting it; you know where to invest your wealth, with whom to entrust it, how none of your gathering need be lost. Well, I ask you in your shrewdness and carefulness: Granted your gathering and storing are proof against any loss, tell me for whom you store your treasure. There are other evils that go with this vanity of your covetousness; those are not my concern at this moment; I neither stress them nor tax you with them. The one point I make,

---

13. LXX; Psalm 39 elsewhere. Translations of this and the following texts are mine.

the one question I put, is what is brought up by the reading of the Psalm. Granted, you gather and lay up treasure. I do not say: "Beware, that in gathering you should not be gathered up yourself; beware, that greed may not have dulled your hearing or understanding"; I will put it more plainly. I do not say, then: "Beware, that in your zeal to prey on the lesser, you become the prey of the greater; unwittingly, unbeknown to yourself, you live in a sea where the bigger fish eat up the smaller." I pass that by; I pass by the difficulties and dangers that beset the quest for money, the trials of those who gather it, the risks that they face at every turn, the mortal fears that haunt them continually; and this I pass by. Granted, you gather wealth unopposed, you store it unmolested. But examine that shrewdness, that wisdom which emboldens you to deride my words and account them folly; then tell me; you lay up treasure; for whom do you think to gather it? I see what you mean to answer (do you think it escaped the psalmist?); you will tell me, "My children; I am storing it for them." To screen your iniquity you make a plea of paternal love—the excuse of injustice. "I am storing it for my children." Granted you are; did not Idithun (Jeduthun)[14] know about this? He certainly knew it, but held such things to belong to the old dayd, and spurred them because he was hastening towards the new.

12. I return to probe this matter of you and your children. You who store and they whom you store for are doomed to pass away; or rather (for "doomed to pass" implies some permanence now), you and they are already passing. Take this very day; from the sermon's opening words to this moment we have been growing older, though you are not conscious of it. So with the hair of your head; it grows unnoticed, but grow it does—now in church, while you are standing there, while you say or do anything; there is no sudden growth of it to send you to the barber's. Thus in all of us time goes fleeting by, whether our mind is on it, whether it is occupied elsewhere, or whether

---

14. One of the three directors of music of the temple service appointed by David; see 1 Chron 16:41–42; 25:1–6. Along with this Psalm 38 (LXX; elsewhere 39), his name stands at the head of Psalms 62 and 77.

it may be with something evil. You are passing away, and the son you store for is passing too. Hence I ask you first: this son you store for—are you sure he will inherit? And again, if he is not yet born, are you sure he will be? You store for children who may never be born or never inherit; your treasure is stored, but not in its rightful place.

You are servant to a great estate owner; as such you have also been entrusted goods of your own; and your master's advice could never mean the loss of his servant's goods. All that you have and love was given to you by him, and he would not have you lose his own gift, since indeed he is ready to give you himself. Moreover, he would not have you lose even his temporal gift. There is plenty of it, it is overflowing, it may surely deem to have reached excess; even so, says your master, "I would not have you lose it." "What then am I to do?" Remove it; the place you have stored it is unsafe. If you consult your own covetousness even, you may find that my counsel satisfies it, too. You wish to keep what you have already without loss; I am showing you where you may secure it. Do not lay up treasure on earth, not knowing for whom you gather it or how its owner and keeper may squander it. The person who possesses it may be possessed by someone else; or while you store it for him you may lose it yourself before he comes.

Hence I counsel you in your anxiety: "Lay up for yourselves treasures in heaven" [Matt 6:20]. If you wished to guard wealth here on earth, you would look for a storehouse; you might mistrust your own house because of the servants; you might take your goods to the banking quarter, where accidents are less likely, thieves can scarcely get in, and everything is securely guarded. Yet why should you take this measure except that you have no better storehouse? What if I offer you a better one? This will be my advice: "Do not commit your goods to the banker, he is not to be trusted; there is another whom you may trust, commit them to him. He has great storehouses where wealth can never be lost; he is rich beyond all the rich." At this you will say perhaps: "I will never dare to ask such a one to guard my goods." But what if he invites you? Know him for who he is; this person of great estate is your own Lord, and he speaks thus: "My servant, I would not have you lose your goods; learn from me where to store them. Why keep them where you may lose them, and where you yourself cannot permanently live? There is another place; I will take you there. Let your wealth go ahead of you; fear no loss; I who gave it will guard it for you."

Such are your Lord's words. Question your faith; will you trust him? You will say: "What I cannot see is as good as lost; I must see my wealth here." But if you insist it, you will neither see it here nor possess anything there. You have treasures—no matter what—buried underground; when you leave the house you do not take them with you. You came here to hear a sermon, to reap some spiritual wealth, but your thoughts are with the temporal; well, have you actually brought it with you? Well, at this very moment you cannot see it. You think you have it at home, where you know you have put it, but are you sure that you have not lost it? Many people before now have gone home and not found what they had hoarded. Did some covetous hearts beat faster then? When I spoke of returning to emptied stock, I think there was a whispering in each of them: "Heaven forbid, Bishop; wish us better fortune; say a prayer for us; heaven forbid such disaster should happen; I trust in God that I shall find my treasure safe." You trust in God then, and do not trust God himself? "I trust in Christ that what I left will be safe and sound, that none will go near it, none will take it." If you trust in Christ, you think you need to fear no loss at home; in fact, you need to fear nothing if you indeed trust him and store your goods where he counsels you. Are you sure of your servant and doubtful of your Lord, sure of your house and doubtful of heaven? "But I," you ask me, "how can I put treasure in heaven?" You have heard my counsel; store your treasure where I have said; I do not want you to know how it reaches heaven. Put it in the hands of the poor; give it to those in need; what does it matter to you how it reaches there? Will I not deliver what I receive? Have you forgotten my words:

"When you have done it to one of the least of mine, you have done it unto me" [Matt 25:40]?

Suppose that some friend of yours had vats, cisterns, or other containers skillfully made for storing wine or oil; and suppose yourself in search of somewhere to hide or store your produce. He might say to you: "I will store it for you." He would have secret channels and passages to the containers, and through them the liquid visibly poured would travel invisibly. Again, he might say to you: "Pour out here what you have"; and you, finding that this was not the place where you thought to put it, might be afraid to pour. But your friend, knowing the hidden workings beneath his grounds, would surely bid you: "Pour it and set your mind at rest; it passes from here to there; you cannot see how, but you may trust me; I am the builder."

He by whom all things were made has built mansions for all of us; and lest we should lose our goods on earth, he would have them go before us there. If you store them on earth, tell me for whom you gather them. You have children, you answer. Number one more among them; let one portion be Christ's.

Sermons

206: On Lent

1. With the completion of the year's cycle, the season of Lent has come; in light of that, I am obligated to exhort you because you owe the Lord works in harmony with the spirit of the season, works which, nonetheless, are useful not to the Lord, but to you. True, other seasons of the year should glow for the Christians by their prayers, fasts, and alms deeds; but this season must arouse even those who are sluggish at other times. In fact, those who are quick to attend to these works at other times should now perform them with even greater diligence. Life in this world is certainly the time of our humiliation as these days signify when the sufferings of the Lord Christ, who once suffered by dying for us, are renewed each year with the recurrence of this holy season. For what was done once and for

all so that our life might be renewed, is solemnly celebrated each year so that its memory may be kept fresh. If, therefore, we ought to be humble of heart with most sincere piety throughout the entire period of our earthly sojourn when we live in the midst of temptations, how much more necessary is humility during these days when we not only pass the time of our humiliation by living, but manifest it by special devotion? Christ's humility has taught us to be humble because he yielded to the wicked by accepting his death; the exaltation of Christ lifts us up because by rising again he blazed the way for his devoted followers. For "if we have died with him, we will also live with him; if we endure, we will also reign with him" [2 Tim 2:11–13]. One of these conditions we now celebrate with due observance in view of his approaching Passion; the other we will celebrate after Easter when his resurrection is, as it were, accomplished again. Then, after the days of this humiliation will be the time of our glorification. Although now is not yet the time to experience this exaltation, it gives us pleasure to anticipate it in our considerations. Now, therefore, let us voice our lamentations more insistently in prayers; then we will rejoice more exuberantly in praise.

2. Let us by our prayers add the wings of piety to our almsgiving and fasting so that they may fly more readily to God. Moreover, the Christian soul understands how much one should avoid stealing another's goods when he realizes that failure to share his surplus with the needy is like a theft. The Lord says: "Give, and it will be given to you; forgive, and you will be forgiven" [Luke 6:37–38]. Let us graciously and fervently perform these two types of almsgiving, that is, giving and forgiving, for we, in turn, pray the Lord to give us good things and not to repay our evil deeds. "Give, and it will be given to you," he says. What is truer, what is more just, than that those who refuse to give should cheat themselves and not receive? If a farmer is not justified in gathering a harvest when he knows he has sowed no seed, how much more unreasonable for him who has refused to hear the petition of a poor man to expect a generous response from God? In the person of the poor, he who

experiences no hunger wished himself to be fed. Therefore, let us not spurn our God who is needy in his poor, so that we in our need may be filled in him who is rich. We have the needy, and we ourselves have need; let us give, therefore, so that we may receive. In truth, what is it that we give? And in return for that trifle which is meager, visible, temporal, and earthly, what do we desire to receive? What the "eye has not seen nor ear heard, nor has it entered into the heart of people" [1 Cor 2:4]. Without the assurance of God it would have been arrogance to wish to gain such treasures in return for such paltry trifles; and it is arrogance to refuse to give to our needy neighbor these things, which we would never have possessed except for the bounty of God who urges us to give. With what confidence do we hope to see him giving to our neighbor and to us, if we despise his commands in the least details? "Forgive, and you will be forgiven," that is, pardon and you will be pardoned. Let servant be reconciled to fellow servant let he is justly punished by the Lord. In this kind of almsgiving no one is poor. Even one who has no means of livelihood in this world may do this to insure one's living for eternity. You give these alms gratuitously; you increase them by giving them away; and they are not exhausted except when they are not shared. Therefore, let those lasting enmities even to this day be broken up and ended. Let them be ended lest they end you; let them be no longer held lest they hold you; let them be destroyed by the Redeemer lest they destroy you, the keeper.

3. Let not your fasting be of the kind condemned by the prophet when God said: "Is not this fast have I chosen, says the Lord?" [Isa 58:5]. He denounces the fasts of quarrelers and seeks those of the devout. He denounces those who oppress and seeks those who release. He denounces those who stir up hostilities and seeks those who set free. For, during these days, you restrain your desires from lawful pursuits that you may not do what is unlawful. At no time will one be addicted to wine or adultery who is now continent in marriage. Thus, by humility and charity, by fasting and almsgiving, by temperance and forgiveness, by sharing blessings and by not retaliat-

ing for evils, by declining from wickedness and by doing good, our prayer seeks and attains peace. For prayer, supported as it were on the wings of virtues, speeds upwards and is easily borne into heaven, to which Christ, our peace, has preceded.

239: On the Resurrection of Christ

4. If Elijah needed nothing [cf. 1 Kgs 17:9–17], did Christ need anything? My beloved, the Scriptures admonish us for this very reason: God frequently brings need upon his servants, whom he is able to feed, so that he may find devoted souls. Let no one be proud because they give to the poor; Christ was poor. Let no one be proud because they receive a wanderer; Christ was a wanderer. The One received is better the one who offers hospitality. The One who accepts is richer than those who give. He who received possessed all things; those who gave offered to Christ from whom they had received what he gave. Let none of you, then, be proud when you give to the poor, my beloved. You should not say in your mind: "I give, he accepts; I receive him, he needs shelter." Perhaps he is superior to you in some respect in ways you are lacking. Perhaps he whom you receive is just; he lacks bread, but you lack truth; he lacks a roof, but you lack heaven; he lacks money, but you lack justice.

Lend your money; pay out what you receive. Do not be afraid that God will judge you if you lend your money. By all means, by all means, lend your money. But God says to you: "What do you wish?" Do you wish to exact usury? What does "to exact usury" mean? To give less and receive more. Then God says to you: "Behold, give to me; I receive less and I give more. What do I say? Yes, I give a hundredfold and life everlasting." The one to whom you seek to give your money so that it may increase, the man whom you thus seek, rejoices when he gets the money and weeps when he returns it; he begs to get the money, but he slanders you to avoid repaying it. Yes, indeed, give to the man and do not turn away from him who seeks a loan. But take only so much as you have given. Let him to whom you have given not weep; otherwise, you have spoiled an act of kindness.

And if what you gave and what he received is due and he, perhaps, does not have it at hand, just as you gave it to him when he asked for it, so now wait since he does not have it; he will pay you when he does have it. Do not make new troubles for him whose burdens you once lightened. Look, you have given money, and now you are demanding it; but he does not have the money to give to you. He will pay you when he does have it. Do not shout and say: "Am I asking for a loan? I am seeking only what I gave; what I have given, that I will get back."

You are right; but he does not have the money. You are not a money-lender, yet you want him, to whom you furnished the money, to have recourse to a money-lender in order to pay you. If you are not making your demand because of the interest, so that you may not be regarded as a moneylender, why do you want him to put up with another moneylender because of you? You are putting pressure on him; you are tightening your hold on him even though you are demanding only what you gave. Moreover, by stifling him and by making difficulties for him, you have not shown a kindness but, instead, you have brought much distress upon him. Perhaps, you may say: "He has the resources to pay. He has a home; let him sell it. He has possessions; let him sell them." When he sought help from you, he did so in order not to sell; let him not, because of your demand, do what you helped him to avoid. God orders and God wills that this attitude be taken toward all people.

5. But are you avaricious? God says to you: "Be avaricious! Be just as avaricious as you can, but come to terms with Me, for I made my rich Son poor for your sake." Truly, when Christ was rich, he became poor on account of us [cf. 2 Cor 8:9]. Do you seek gold? He made it. Do you seek silver? He made it. Do you seek a household? He made it. Do you seek flocks? He made them. Do you seek possessions? He made them. Why do you seek only what he made? Seek him who made all these things. Consider how he loved you: "All things were made through him, and without him nothing was made" [John 1:3]. All things, Christ himself among them, were made by him. He who made all things was himself made among them. He who made

humanity was himself made human; he was made what he made, so that what he made might not perish. He who made all things was made among all things. Consider riches; what is richer than he by whom all things were made? Yet, although he was rich, he took mortal flesh in a virgin's womb. He was born as an infant; he was wrapped in swaddling clothes; he was laid in a manger; he patiently waited for the normal periods of life; he, by whom all seasons were made, patiently endured the seasons. He was nursed; he cried; he appeared as an infant. He lay there, yet he was reigning; he was in the manger, yet he sustained the world; he was nursed by his mother and adored by the Gentiles; he was nursed by his mother and adored by angels; he was nursed by his mother, and announced by a gleaming star. Such riches and such poverty! Riches, that you might be created; poverty, that you might be redeemed. Therefore, the fact that he as a poor man was granted hospitality, as a poor man was the result of the condescension of the recipient, not of the wretchedness of the needy.

13

Leo the Great

Sermon 10[1] (November 444)

1. Beloved, observing the ordinances of the apostolic tradition, we exhort you with pastoral care for the flock. Let us celebrate with the zeal of religious practice the day which our predecessors cleansed from ungodly superstitions and sanctified to works of mercy. Let us show that the authority of the Fathers still lives among us and that their teaching abides in our obedience. Such a great ordinance was not intended to be useful for holiness in the past alone, but in our times as well. What helped them for uprooting empty superstitions can profit us with increases in virtue. What could be more suitable to faith, what more helpful to compassion, than alleviating the poverty of the needy, undertaking care of the sick, succoring needs of the brothers and sisters, and remembering our own condition in the distress of others?

In this undertaking, God alone can discern how much any-

---

1. Translations of the selected sermons are mine.

one can and cannot do [cf. Tob 4:8], and knows what he has given and to whom he has given it. For not only are spiritual provisions and heavenly gifts received through God's bounty, but earthly and material resources also proceed from his largess. God has every right to ask for an accounting of these things, since he gave them more by way of entrusting them to be spent rather than of handing them over to be kept [cf. Acts 20:35]. We must therefore use the gifts of God with justice and prudence so that the opportunity for a good work does not become an occasion of sin. Riches are good in and of themselves. They offer many advantages to human society when they are in the hands of generous benefactors—but not when some extravagant person shows them off or some miser hides them away. Whether hoarded or foolishly spent, they equally go to waste.

2. It would indeed be praiseworthy to flee intemperance and to avoid the wastes that would result from unworthy desires. Many magnanimous souls find it repugnant to hide their wealth and, overflowing with abundance, they recoil from mean and sordid parsimony. Yet an abundance of such things cannot be considered prosperous nor frugality commended if their riches are at the service of themselves alone, if no poor are assisted by their goods, if no sick are taken care of, if no captive sees ransom from the abundance of their means, no stranger comfort, no exile relief. Rich people like these are poorer than any of the poor. They forfeit those eternal revenues that are within their power to obtain. Resting upon a short-lived and not always free enjoyment of their possessions, they fail to nourish themselves at all on the savory food of justice and mercy. They are splendid on the outside but murky within. Abounding in temporal things, they are impoverished of things eternal. Those who from what they have put into earthly storehouses have put nothing into the heavenly treasures inflict starvation on their own souls and put them to shame with nakedness.

3. But perhaps there are some rich people who, though they are not in the habit of helping the poor in the church with their

largess, still keep other commandments of God and think that among the various meritorious activities of faith they are lacking only one virtue—and it is therefore a slight fault. Yet this one virtue is so important that without it their other virtues can be of no avail. Be any full of faith, chaste, sober, and adorned with other noteworthy decorations, yet if they are not merciful, they cannot deserve mercy. For the Lord says, "Blessed are the merciful, for God will have mercy on them" [Matt 5:7]. When the Son of man will come in his majesty and sit on the throne of his glory, when all nations are gathered together, the good and the bad will be separated. For what will those who stand on the right be praised if not the works of benevolence and deeds of charity that Jesus Christ will consider as rendered unto himself [cf. Matt 25:31–46]? That is because in making human nature his own he has not dissociated himself from any aspect of human lowliness. What will be the accusations against those on the left if not neglect of love, inhuman harshness, and denying compassion to the poor? It is as if those on the right would have no other virtues, those on the left no other offenses! But at that great and final Judgment, the kindness of generosity or the ungodliness of avarice will receive such a high value as to outweigh all other virtues and all other faults. Thus, some will be accepted into heaven on account of that one good, but others will be cast into eternal fire on account of that one evil.

4. Therefore, let no one, dearly beloved, flatter themselves about any merits of living a good life if they lack the works of charity. Nor should people be complacent about the purity of their bodies if they have not "been cleansed" at all by the purification "of alms" [cf. Luke 11:41]. Alms wipe away sins, destroy death, and extinguish the punishment of eternal fire [cf. Prov 10:12; 15:27; 16:6; Dan 4:24; Tob 4:11–12; Sir 3:33; 1 Pet 4:8]. But those who are without its fruit will be strangers to the mercy of the great Recompenser, as Solomon says: "Whoever closes one's ears so as not to hear the week, will themselves call upon the Lord and likewise find no one to hear them" [Prov 21:13]. So Tobias as well, instructing his son in the precepts of

religions, says: "Give alms from your possessions and do not turn your face away from any poor person; so shall the face of God not be turned away from you either" [Tob 4:7].

This virtue makes all other virtues profitable. It gives life even to faith itself—"by which the just live" [cf. Hab 2:4; Rom 1:17; Gal 3:11; Heb 10:38], and which is called "dead without works" [Jas 2:17, 20, 26]; for as works find their basis in faith, so faith finds its strength in works. "While we have time, then, let us perform good works for everyone, but especially for those who belong to the household of faith," as the Apostle says [Gal 6:10]. "Let us not grow weary of doing good, for in due time we shall reap" [Gal 6:9]. And so this present life is a time for sowing, and the Day of Judgment the time for harvest [cf. Matt 13:30, 39], when all will reap the fruit of their sowing according to the amount of their sowing [cf. 2 Cor 9:6]. Let no one get the wrong impression about this yield of that harvesting; it is the heart in giving rather than the sums expended that will be reckoned. Meager amounts given from meager resources will produce as much as great amounts given from great resources.

Beloved, let us therefore fulfill this apostolic institution. Since Sunday is the anniversary of the first collection, let all be prepared to make a "free-will" donation so that all according to their means may join in this most holy offering. The alms themselves and those who benefit from your gifts will pray for you [cf. Sir 29:15], that you may always be prepared for every good work [cf. 2 Cor 9:8], in Christ Jesus our Lord who lives and reigns for ever and ever without end. Amen.

Sermon 17 (December 17, 444)

1. The teaching of the law, dearly beloved, provides much strength to the commands of the Gospel, seeing that certain things are transferred from the old precepts to the new. We see from the very devotion of the Church that the Lord Jesus "did not come to destroy the law but to fulfill it" [Matt 5:17]. The signs have ceased by which the coming of our Savior had been announced; the figures have been brought to completion

and thus abolished by the presence of the Truth. But things established by piety for the regulation of customs or for the sincere worship of God, continue with us in the same form in which they had been established; and the ordinances fitting to either Testament are not changed by any alteration. Among these is the solemn fast of the tenth month, which by yearly custom we are to keep now; for it is altogether just and godly to give thanks to the divine bounty for the fruits which the earth has yielded for human use, under the guidance of the supreme Providence. In order to show that we are acting with a willing heart, it is necessary that we take on not only the self-restraint of the fast but also the diligence of almsgiving. That way, the seed of righteousness and the fruit of charity might also spring up from the ground of our heart.

We may deserve the mercy of God by showing mercy to his poor. The most effective prayer to make requests of God is that which is supported by the works of mercy, since those who do not turn away their hearts from the poor quickly turn the Lord's ear to themselves, as the Lord says: "Be merciful just as your Father is merciful; forgive and you will be forgiven" [Luke 6:36–37]. What is more gracious than this justice? What is more merciful than this recompense, where the judge's sentence rests in the power of the one to be judged? "Give and it will be given to you" [Luke 6:38], he says. How quickly this takes away hesitant anxiety and delaying avarice so that a confident compassion may give away what the Truth promises to repay!

2. Be steadfast then, Christian giver. Give what you receive, sow what you reap, scatter what you collect. Do not fear the cost, do not sigh over a doubtful gain. Your property increases when it is well spent. Set your heart on the just reward of mercy and pursue the business of the eternal gain. Your Benefactor wants you to be beneficent, and he who gives that you may have, entrusts it so that you may distribute it, saying: "Give and it will be given to you" [Luke 6:38]. You must gratefully embrace the condition of this promise. For although you have nothing that you have not received, you cannot but have

what you have given away. Consequently, those who love money and hope to increase their wealth with immoderate profits, let them rather practice this holy usury and grow rich by this art of money-lending, that they should not trade on the necessities of laboring people and entrap them in impossible debts through deceitful benefits. Let them instead be the creditors and the money-lenders of someone who said: "Give and it will be given to you," and "the measure with which you measure, the same will be measured back to you" [Luke 6:38].

But those are unfaithful and even unjust to themselves, who do not want to have forever what they value worthy of their love. However much they add to their wealth, however much they store and accumulate, they will leave this world helpless and needy, as David the prophet said: "For when he dies he will take nothing away, nor shall his glory descend with him" [Ps 49:17 (48:16 LXX)]. If any would be kind to their own souls, they should entrust their goods to him who is a faithful trustee of the poor and a most generous payer of interest. But an unrighteous and shameless greed, which, pretending to offer a benefit while it deceives them, does not trust God whose promise never fails, and yet trusts people who make such hasty bargain. While they regard the present more certain than the future, they often and deservedly find that the desire of unjust gain is the cause of a not unjust loss.

3. Whatever the outcome, the system of usury is always evil since it is sin either to lessen or increase the money. Either people are miserable in losing what they gave, or they are more miserable still when receiving what they did not give. Therefore, the evil of usury must be shunned, and the gain that lacks all humanity must be avoided. One's wealth indeed multiplies by unjust and grievous gains, but the soul's wealth decays, since usury in money is the death of the soul. The holy prophet David shows what God thinks about such people when he says: "Lord, who will dwell in your tabernacle, or who will rest on your holy mountain" [Ps 14:1]? He is instructed by the reply of the divine voice, and learns that people gain eternal rest if, among other rules of a holy life, "they do not give their own

money at usury" [Ps 14:1]. Those who seize a deceitful profit for their money by usury are shown to be strangers to God's tabernacle and foreign to his holy mountain; while they want to become rich by another's loss, they are worthy to be punished by eternal poverty.

4. So you, dearly beloved, who have believed the promises of the Lord with your whole heart, flee the unclean leprosy of avarice and use God's gifts with piety and wisdom. Since you enjoy his generosity, take care that you have those who may share in your joy. For many lack what you have in plenty; and in their need you have been given the means of imitating the divine goodness, so that through you God's gifts may pass to others and that you may acquire eternal goods by wisely dispensing your temporal goods. On next Wednesday and Friday, therefore, let us fast and on Saturday keep vigil with the most blessed Apostle Peter, by whose prayers we may in all things obtain the divine protection through Christ our Lord. Amen.

14

Rabbula of Edessa

The Heroic Deeds of Mar Rabbula[1]

As soon as the blessed Rabbula was baptized and went back to his city and entered his home, he made preparations as he had vowed. He was like a wise merchant who set forth after precious pearls. When the merchant found the pearl of his hope, he went and sold whatever he had and brought it [Matt 13:45]. So Rabbula distributed to the needy his gold and his silver and all that he possessed; his alms extended even as far as to the saints and the poor in Edessa. This act foretold that he would receive the city of Edessa as his inheritance.[2] For the mystery of Christ had in advance espoused him to Edessa, as to the rest of the regions, with his alms as a pledge, through the agency of her wedding-attendants, the poor. For he wisely understood

---

1. Translation comes from Robert Doran, trans. and intro., *Stewards of the Poor: The Man of God, Rabbula, and Hiba in Fifth Century Edessa* (Kalamazoo, MI: Cistercian, 2006), 71–72, 76–78, 85–86. Copyright © 2006 by Cistercian Publications. Copyright © 2008 by Order of Saint Benedict, Collegeville, Minnesota. Used with permission.
2. That is, the church. See the connection between mystery, Christ, and the church in Eph 5:32; Col 1:27; 2:2.

in his soul that the decorations of this world and the anxiety of riches, like briars and thorns, choke the seed of the word of God in the unwary, and it does not produce fruits [cf. Matt 13:3–9]. Because of this, he labored to hurl from himself all the hard burden of the chains of riches [cf. Matt 19:16–30], so that the word of God that he received might easily sprout up within him and yield fruits thirtyfold and sixtyfold and a hundredfold [Matt 13:18–23; Mark 4:3–20]. Thus with joy he accepted the command of our Lord: "Whosoever does not leave behind al his possessions cannot be my disciple" [Luke 12:13–21; 14:26–27, 33]. He diligently distributed and gave all that he had to the poor so that his righteousness would stand firm forever. He even sold his estates and he properly distributed to the needy the money he received from their sale, so that, by means of them, his deposits to the heavenly treasury, along with their profits, might mount up. There his treasures would be kept safe for him. He set free all his slaves, both those born in the hours and those bought by money, and he provisioned and sent away in peace each and every one of them. He instructed, taught, and brought some of them to the monasteries. As for his blessed mother, she rejoiced when he took all that she possessed, and then she took the yoke of Christ. He did likewise to his wife. He taught his till young children, and entrusted them to the monasteries. Thus he emptied himself of all that he had possessed so that he might possess the Lord of all possessions.

When he had separated himself according to the command of our Lord from his mother and from his wife and from his sons and his daughters and from his estates and from all his possessions and from the villages dependent on him and from his slaves and from his friends and from all that the world possesses [cf. Matt 19:29], according to the command of our Lord he took up his cross in secret manner [Matt 10:38; 16:24; Mark 8:34; Luke 9:23; 14:27], and set out after him completely. As soon as he had stripped off the world, with its life and all that is in it, he set out alone for the desert in the glowing desire for the true love of Christ, so that he also might be tested by the slanderer as by the example of our Lord [cf. Matt 4:1–11;

Mark 1:12–13; Luke 4:1–13]. He desired, like a warrior in the field, to encounter battles with the fierce passions, to strive in a wrestling match with his nature and its habits, and, like a spiritual athlete, to contend with principalities and with powers and with evil spirits, from within and without [cf. 1 Cor 10:3–4; Gal 6:16–17; Eph 1:21; 6:10–20; 1 Tim 4:7–8].

So he went and dwelt in the desert monastery of the blessed Abraham, whom we mentioned above. The blessed Rabbula had been drawn at the beginning, by the small radiance of one of Abraham's signs, to leave the darkness of paganism for the light of the truth. When Rabbula had lived with him for some time in a noble way of life, he strongly urged Abraham that he might take for himself a small dwelling-place near Abraham and live in it as he pleased. So Abraham assented to his argument, and Rabbula took up residence in the monastery. . . . When he saw that people were beginning to visit him as someone who had left behind the world and desired solitude, who hated himself and love God, he concealed himself from them so that he might not be hindered by their visits from his steady regime of righteousness. He removed himself to the inner desert, as also the blessed Anthony had done [Athanasius, *Life of Anthony*, 49]. . . .

When my lord Diogenes, bishop of Edessa, passed away, the bishops, with Alexander the patriarch, gathered at Antioch along with Acacius, bishop of Aleppo, to consider whom they might appoint bishop of Edessa. The spirit[3] of Jesus allowed in their hearts, "It is right to elect Rabbula for that place because I delight in him" [Isa 42:1]. The spirit, by the mouth of priests, said about Rabbula what it had about David, "I have found Rabbula my servant who will be useful in my service. I will anoint him with the old of my holiness by your hand" [1 Sam 16:12–13; Acts 13:22]. . . .

Now, when Edessa heard the news of the priesthood of its pastor, Rabbula, they hastened to go out to meet him in gladness, and they received him in peace. When he entered [the city] and sat upon the throne of the priest, all the people of

---

3. "Spirit" here is feminine.

Edessa applauded him greatly and acclaimed him with their voices. From the first he demonstrated his excellent diligence concerning the previous rules of the liturgy of the church. . . .

By the wisdom of God within him, he translated the new covenant from Greek to Syriac, exactly as it was, on account of its various alterations. He straightaway ordered that many silver vessels, which had been fashioned with care for the serving of ten tables of clerics, be sold. He distributed equitably the price they fetched for the use of the needy. He gently persuaded the clerics to use clay vessels. He also determined to sell the liturgical vessels of silver and gold which the churches had and to give the prices they fetched to the poor, as he said, "It is clear to those who know that adorned liturgical vessels of gold and silver are not especially necessary for the glory of God, but that the spirit of God rests in pure hearts." Yet his order was neglected because of their contempt. At the request of many he was restrained from doing this because the vessels were the offerings of their earlier, now deceased, fathers, who had offered them to God for the redemption of their spirit.

He exhorted his clergy like a father to his own sons and instructed them like a head to its members. . . . "Except because of the necessity of illness or the distress of pain, abstain completely from flesh and fowl, along with bathing; not even in the case of ordinary food should you have concern for an abundance of bodily nourishment lest its pleasure smite you with pestering desires. Let the love of silver or the desire for possessions, something foreign to our ways, not even be mentioned among you. Let not fine clothing or elegant garments diminish the honor of your modesty, but instead of these may you persevere in fasts and prayers and in holy deeds." . . .

Now those members of his monastery, with all his own clergy, were always bound to him by the word of God so that they would accept absolutely nothing from people in the likeness of a present or an honorarium. He even made all the priests of his diocese subject at all times to the punishment of suspension, so that they would not dare to bring anything at all to one of his companions or to one from all his clergy. "In the case that they bring us a present calling it a blessings, we, who are held in honor by them, rightly should give [the blessings]. In the case of an honorarium, this is a mockery as we, who possess the authority, appropriately confer honor. But in the case of a gift from compulsion, we who would be supported by them, should have no part [in such a transaction]. Therefore, on every count it is we who are under an obligation to give, and not to receive."

What monk can be compared to him as regards his high degree of privation? In mind he was a monk, and his habitual clothing was a hair tunic and a modest mantle. At the liturgy of the church, he used to wear in winter the one cloak he possessed, and, in summer, one sleeveless vestment. His humble bedding consisted only of a mat, a coverlet, and under his head a small pillow cut from a monk's cloak sufficed. . . .

Not only was he like Paul in these matters[4] but also as regards the great favor which was entrusted to Paul by the earlier apostles to take care of the poor.[5] Rabbula was concerned to perform this service too. He kept it as diligently as if he, along with Paul, had received from the apostles this commandment to care for the poor. Who can relate the great care he had for the sustenance of the poor, especially the lofty love he possessed for the poor holy ones? Now, each of the solitary dwelling-places of the monasteries of pious men—who steadily lived the life of recluse and whose bones, even after their departure were a sweet fragrance in Christ—possessed, at this command, a solitary cell for him. He wished that, as often as he came to visit them, he might be helped in his faith by those who had fallen asleep in peace and especially that he might help their disciples with his exhortations. In the cell he would silently dwell alone to persevere in prayer acceptable to God and so that his prayer might profit him. Although many and frequent were the offerings of his alms to all people at all times, he also particularly desired to offer himself as a sacrifice to Christ on behalf of all people. According to the desire

4. In experiencing sufferings and afflictions.
5. Acts 11:29–30; 24:17; Rom 15:26; 1 Cor 16:1–4; 2 Cor 8:1–4; 9:1; Gal 2:9–10.

of his good will towards God and people, he supported his fellow poor out of what belonged to his Lord for as long as he lived in the world according to the will of God. Even after his departure, he left them a good inheritance of prayer, and he entrusted them to the grace of God, the mother of all, so that, from her,[6] the necessity of their needs might be fully supplied every day. Because the fire of love for Rabbula lives on in their hearts, and the precious memory of the beloved name of Rabbula is preserved, her support and her flame reflect the fire of love in their hearts. Because of this, all the needy obtain the supply of their necessities through his good name, as from a gracious fullness. As soon as his friends hear the sweet name of Rabbula, love of him is inflamed in their hearts. Their compassion bubbles up and they give alms. The recipient rejoices, and the giver is helped, and God is praised as, in this way, the work of our father Rabbula towards his Lord is preserved. . . .

Because of the love of the poor which he had in his soul, he worked an excellent change in the hospital of his city. What before had been nominally but not really [a hospital] he deemed truly worthy to be [supported] for the glory of God, and to serve appropriately to honor God. He set apart for the hospital certain estates from the wealth of his church so that, from their harvests, what the hospital expended in order to exist might be provided. An opportunity was provided to many to leave riches and property to the hospital in their wills, so that, from them, a thousand *denarii* might be the total income for the hospital in one year. Thus, there was relief for the weak and benefits for the healthy through the provision of his word. Who was there from those whose conscience was foul who did not earnestly desire to feed from the variety of meals for the sick provided through the diligence of his decree? It was impossible for someone to have known through [any sign of] negligence that the sick and those smitten with sores had been placed there, because of the care and the cleanliness upon them by his decree. For their beds were pleasant with soft bedding placed upon them; no dirty or vile linen was there, or ever

6. Here grace is personified, and, as "grace" is a feminine noun, it is seen as feminine.

seen upon them. Trustworthy and truly caring deacons were put in charge by him for the relief their ministration brought and for the provision of what was needed. . . .

For the love of God, which blazed and burnt like a fire compassionately for his fellow human beings, he especially manifested his great care upon the poor lepers who dwelt in isolation outside the city, hated and despised. He put in charge of them a steadfast deacon, who dwelt beside them, with trustworthy brethren appointed to minister to them. Everything necessary for their need came continually from the church inside, while Rabbula himself at all times refreshed their souls by action and by word. Through the action of his charismatic gift, he healed the suffering of their diseases; through the word of God he confronted their mind, that it not be choked by distress. How many times, as a comfort to their souls, did he place the peace of a holy kiss upon the rotting lips of men whose bodies were putrefying, and strengthen them so that their mind not lose hope because of the chastisement of God towards them? He urged them to praise our Lord especially because of their afflictions, as he said, "Recall, my brothers, how it is written that Lazarus, because he endured evil, was esteemed worthy to lie down on the bosom of Abraham in the place of the kingdom" [Luke 16:19–31].

Select Bibliography

This bibliography, especially on English translations and secondary works, includes a very select list although there are many full English translations and secondary studies available. Given a limited space available, this select list presents the ones I have directly used and/or major and representative ones with more recent translations.

Primary Sources

Ambrose. *Letter 2*. Pages 14–19 in *Sancti Ambrosii opera, pars decima: epistulæ et acta*, vol. 1: *Epistularum libri I–VI*. Edited by Otto Faller. Corpus scriptorum ecclesiasticorum Latinorum 82. Vienna: Tempsky, 1968.

_____. *On Naboth*. Pages 469–516 in *Sancti Ambrosii opera, pars altera*. Edited by Karl Schenkl. Corpus scriptorum ecclesiasticorum Latinorum 32/2. Vienna: Tempsky, 1897.

_____. *On the Duties of the Clergy*. Columns 23–184 in *Sancti Ambrosii, Mediolanensis episcopi, opera omnia*, vol. 2 pt. 1. Edited by J.-P. Migne. Patrologia Latina 16. Paris: Imprimerie Catholique, 1880.

_____. *On Tobit*. Columns 759–94 in *Sancti Ambrosii, Mediolanensis episcopi, opera omnia*, vol. 1 pt. 1. Edited by J.-P. Migne. Patrologia Latina 14. Paris: Imprimerie Catholique, 1882.

Augustine. *On Christian Doctrine*. Pages 1–167 in *Sancti Aurelii Augustini De doctrina christiana; De vera religione*. Edited by Josef Martin. Corpus Christianorum series Latina 32. Turnhout: Brepols, 1962.

_____. *Exposition on Psalm 38*. In *Sancti Aurelii Augustini Enarrationes in Psalmos I–L*. Edited by E. Dekkers and J. Fraipont. Corpus Christianorum series Latina 38. Turnhout: Brepols, 1956. Repr., 1990.

_____. *Letter 93*. Columns 321–47 in *Sancti Aurelii Augustini, Hipponensis episcopi, opera omnia*, vol. 3 pt. 2. Edited by J.-P. Migne. Patrologia Latina 33. Paris: Imprimerie Catholique, 1865.

_____. *Letter 130*. Columns 494–507 in *Sancti Aurelii Augustini, Hipponensis episcopi, opera omnia*, vol. 3 pt. 2. Edited by J.-P. Migne. Patrologia Latina 33. Paris: Imprimerie Catholique, 1865.

_____. *Letter 153*. Columns 653–65 in *Sancti Aurelii Augustini, Hipponensis episcopi, opera omnia*, vol. 3 pt. 2. Edited by J.-P. Migne. Patrologia Latina 33. Paris: Imprimerie Catholique, 1865.

_____. *Letter 157*. Columns 674–93 in *Sancti Aurelii Augustini, Hipponensis episcopi, opera omnia*, vol. 3 pt. 2. Edited by J.-P. Migne. Patrologia Latina 33. Paris: Imprimerie Catholique, 1865.

_____. *Sermon 206*. Columns 1041–42 in *Sancti Aurelii Augustini, Hipponensis episcopi, opera omnia*, vol. 5 pt. 1. Edited by J.-P. Migne. Patrologia Latina 38. Paris: Imprimerie Catholique, 1861.

_____. *Sermon 239*. Columns 1126–30 in *Sancti Aurelii Augustini, Hipponensis episcopi, opera omnia*, vol. 5 pt. 1. Edited by J.-P. Migne. Patrologia Latina 38. Paris: Imprimerie Catholique, 1861.

_____. *Tractates on the Gospel of John*. Published as *Sancti Aurelii Augustini, In Johannis Evangelium tractatus CXXIV*. Edited by R. Willems. Corpus Christianorum series Latina 36. Turnhout: Brepols, 1954.

Basil. *Homily on Psalm 14: Against Lending with Interest* 1, 5. Columns 265–66 and 277–80 in *Sancti patris nostri Basilii, Cæsareæ Cappadociæ archiepiscopi, opera omnia quæ exstant*, vol. 1. Edited by J.-P. Migne. Patrologia Graeca 29. Paris: Imprimerie Catholique, 1857.

_____. *Homily 6: "I Will Pull Down My Barns."* Columns 261–78 in *Sancti patris nostri Basilii, Cæsareæ Cappadociæ archiepiscopi, opera omnia quæ exstant*, vol. 3. Edited by J.-P. Migne. Patrologia Graeca 31. Paris: Imprimerie Catholique, 1857. Reprint, Turnhout: Brepols, 1977.

_____. *Homily 7: To the Rich*. Columns 277–304 in *Sancti patris nostri Basilii, Cæsareæ Cappadociæ archiepiscopi, opera omnia quæ exstant*, vol. 3. Edited by J.-P. Migne. Patrologia Graeca 31. Paris: Imprimerie Catholique, 1857. Reprint, Turnhout: Brepols, 1977.

_____. *Homily 8: In Time of Famine and Drought*. Columns 303–28 in *Sancti patris nostri Basilii, Cæsareæ Cappadociæ archiepiscopi, opera omnia quæ exstant*, vol. 3. Edited by J.-P. Migne. Patrologia Graeca 31. Paris: Imprimerie Catholique, 1857. Reprint, Turnhout: Brepols, 1977.

_____. *The Shorter Rules*, Question 92. Columns 1146–47 in *Sancti patris nostri Basilii, Cæsareæ Cappadociæ archiepiscopi, opera omnia quæ exstant*, vol. 3. Edited by J.-P. Migne. Patrologia Graeca 31. Paris: Imprimerie Catholique, 1857. Reprint, Turnhout: Brepols, 1977.

Clement of Alexandria. *The Rich Man's Salvation.* Pages 159–91 in *Clemens Alexandrinus*, vol. 3. Edited by Otto Stählin, Ludwig Früchtel, and Ursula Treu. Die griechischen christlichen Schriftsteller der ersten Jahrhunderte 17. Berlin: Akademie, 1970.

Cyprian. *On the Lapsed.* Pages 221–42 in *Sancti Cypriani, episcopi, opera*, vol. 1. Corpus Christianorum series Latina 3. Turnhout: Brepols, 1972.

_____. *On Works and Almsgiving.* Pages 55–72 in *Sancti Cypriani, episcopi, opera*, vol. 2. Corpus Christianorum series Latina 3A. Turnhout: Brepols, 1976.

Gregory of Nazianzus. *Oration 14: On the Love of the Poor.* Columns 857–910 in *Sancti patris nostri Gregorii Theologi, vulgo Nazienzeni, archiepiscopi constantinopolitani, opera quæ exstant omnia*, vol. 1. Edited by J.-P. Migne. Patrologia Graeca 35. Paris: Imprimerie Catholique, 1857.

Gregory of Nyssa. *On the Love of the Poor 1.* Pages 1–37 in *De pauperibus amandis orationes duo.* Edited by Arie van Heck. Leiden: Brill, 1964.

John Chrysostom. *Homilies on the Acts of the Apostles.* Columns 13–384 in *Sancti patris nostri Joannis Chrysostomi, archiepiscopi constantinopolitani, opera omnia quæ exstant*, vol. 9. Edited by J.-P. Migne. Patrologia Graeca 60. Paris: Imprimerie Catholique, 1858–1860. Reprint, Turnhout: Brepols, 1978.

_____. *Homilies on the First Letter to Timothy.* Columns 501–600 in *Sancti patris nostri Joannis Chrysostomi, archiepiscopi constantinopolitani, opera omnia quæ exstant.* Edited by J.-P. Migne. Patrologia Graeca 62. Paris: Imprimerie Catholique, 1860. Reprint, Turnhout: Brepols, 1968.

_____. *Homilies on the Gospel of Matthew.* Published as *Sancti patris nostri Joannis Chrysostomi, archiepiscopi constantinopolitani, opera omnia quæ exstant*, vol. 7 pts. 1–2. Edited by J.-P. Migne. Patrologia Graeca

57–58. Paris: Imprimerie Catholique, 1858–1860. Reprint, Turnhout: Brepols, 1978.

_____. *Homilies on the Letter to the Ephesians.* Columns 9–176 in *Sancti patris nostri Joannis Chrysostomi, archiepiscopi Constantinopolitani, opera omnia quæ exstant*, vol. 11. Edited by J.-P. Migne. Patrologia Graeca 62. Paris: Imprimerie Catholique, 1860. Reprint, Turnhout: Brepols, 1968.

_____. *Homilies on the Rich Man and Lazarus* 2.4. Columns 987–88 in *Sancti patris nostri Joannis Chrysostomi, archiepiscopi constantinopolitani, opera omnia quæ exstant*, vol. 1. Edited by J.-P. Migne. Patrologia Graeca 48. Paris: Imprimerie Catholique, 1862.

_____. *To the People of Antioch* 2.6. Column 43 in *Sancti patris nostri Joannis Chrysostomi, archiepiscopi constantinopolitani, opera omnia quæ exstant*, vol. 2 pt. 1. Edited by J.-P. Migne. Patrologia Graeca 49. Paris: Imprimerie Catholique, 1862. Reprint, Turnhout: Brepols, 1970.

Lactantius. *Divine Institutes.* Columns 111–822 in *Lucii Cæcilii Firmiani Lactantii opera omnia*. Edited by J.-P. Migne. Patrologia Latina 6. Paris: Imprimerie Catholique, 1844.

Leo the Great. *Sermon* 10. In *Sancti Leonis Magni romani pontificis tractatus septem et nonaginta*. Edited by Antoine Chavasse. Corpus Christianorum series Latina 138. Turnhout: Brepols, 1973.

_____. *Sermon* 17. In *Sancti Leonis Magni romani pontificis tractatus septem et nonaginta*. Edited by Antoine Chavasse. Corpus Christianorum series Latina 138. Turnhout: Brepols, 1973.

Shepherd of Hermas. Pages 455–685 in *The Apostolic Fathers: Greek Texts and English Translations*. Translated and introduced by Michael W. Holmes. 3rd ed. Grand Rapids: Baker Academic, 2007.

Shewring, W. ed. *Rich and Poor in Christian Tradition*. London: Burns Oates & Washbourne, 1948.

Tertullian. *Against Marcion.* Pages 441–726 in *Tertulliani opera*, vol. 1: *Opera catholica; Adversus Marcionem*. Edited by A. Kroymann. Corpus Christianorum series Latina 1. Turnhout: Brepols, 1954.

_____. *On Patience.* Pages 299–317 in *Tertulliani opera*, vol. 1: *Opera catholica; Adversus Marcionem*. Edited by J. G. P. Borleffs. Corpus Christianorum series Latina 1. Turnhout: Brepols, 1954.

Anthologies

Courtonne, Yves, ed. and trans. *Saint Basile: Homélies sur la richesse: Édition critique et exégétique.* Paris: Firmin-Didot, 1935.

Lipsius, R. A., and M. Bonnet, eds. *Acta apostolorum apocrypha*, vol. 2/2. Leipzig: Mendelssohn, 1903.

English Translations

Acts of Thomas. In *The Apocryphal New Testament.* Edited and translated by M. R. James. Oxford: Clarendon, 1924.

Boulding, M., trans. and notes. *Expositions of the Psalms.* vol. 2 (33-50). The Works of Saint Augustine: A Translation for the 21st Century. Hyde Park, NY: New City Press, 2000.

Bowen, A., and P. Garnsey, trans. and intro. *Lactantius: Divine Institutes.* Liverpool: Liverpool University Press, 2003.

Daley, B. E. "Oration 14," in *Gregory of Nazianzus.* The Early Church Fathers. London & New York: Routledge, 2006.

Davidson, I. J., ed. and trans. Ambrose: *De officiis.* 2 vols. Oxford: Oxford University Press, 2001.

Deferrari, R. J., trans. and intro. *Saint Cyprian: Treatises.* The Fathers of the Church 36. New York: Fathers of the Church, 1958.

Doran, Robert, trans. and intro. *Stewards of the Poor: The Man of God, Rabbula, and Hiba in Fifth Century Edessa.* Kalamazoo, MI: Cistercian, 2006.

Eliott, J. K. *The Apocryphal New Testament.* Oxford: Clarendon, 1993.

Evans, E., ed. and trans. *Tertullian: Adversus Marcionem.* 5 vols. Oxford Early Christian Text. Oxford: Clarendon, 1972.

Freeland, J. P., and A. J. Conway, trans. *Leo the Great: Sermons.* The Fathers of the Church 93. Washington, DC: The Catholic University Press of America Press, 1996.

Hill, E., trans. and intro. *Sermons.* Vol. 6 (184-229). The Works of Saint Augustine: A Translation for the 21st Century. Hyde Park, NY: New City Press, 1993.

Holman, S. R. Pages 183-206 in *The Hungry Are Dying: Beggars and Bishops in Roman Cappadocia.* Oxford Studies in Historical Theology. Oxford: Oxford University Press, 2001: Basil of Caesarea, "In Time of

Famine and Drought"; Gregory of Nyssa, "On the Love of the Poor"; Gregory of Nazianzus, "On the Love of the Poor."

Phan, Peter C., trans. and intro. *Social Thought.* Message of the Fathers of the Church 20. Wilmington, DE: Glazier, 1984.

Ramsey, B. "On Naboth," in *Ambrose.* The Early Church Fathers. London & New York: Routledge, 1997.

Roth, Catherine P., trans. and intro. *On Wealth and Poverty: St. John Chrysostom.* Crestwood, NY: St. Vladimir's Seminary Press, 1984.

Schroeder, C. Paul, trans. and intro. *On Social Justice: St. Basil the Great.* Crestwood, NY: St. Vladimir's Seminary Press, 2009.

Silvas, A. M. *The Asketikon of St. Basil the Great.* Oxford Early Christian Studies. New York: Oxford University Press, 2005.

Teske, R. J., trans. and intro. *Letters.* Vols. 2 and 3. The Works of Saint Augustine: A Translation for the 21st Century. Hyde Park, NY: New City Press, 2002, 2004.

Womer, Jan L., ed. and trans. *Morality and Ethics in Early Christianity.* Sources of Early Christian Thought. Philadelphia: Fortress, 1987.

Secondary Works

Allen, Paul, Bronwen Neil, and Wendy Mayer. *Preaching Poverty in Late Antiquity: Perceptions and Realities.* Leipzig: Evangelische Verlagsanstalt, 2009.

Anderson, G. *Charity: The Place of the Poor in the Biblical Tradition.* New Haven: Yale University Press, 2013.

Brown, Peter. *Poverty and Leadership in the Later Roman Empire.* Menahem Stern Jerusalem Lectures. Hanover, NH: University Press of New England, 2002.

_____. *The Ransom of the Soul: Afterlife and Wealth in Early Western Christianity.* Cambridge, MA: Harvard University Press, 2015.

_____. *Through the Eye of a Needle: Wealth, the Fall of Rome, and the Making of Christianity in the West, 350–550 AD.* Princeton: Princeton University Press, 2012.

Constanzo, Eric. *Harbor for the Poor: A Missiological Analysis of Almsgiving in the View and Practice of John Chrysostom.* Eugene, OR: Wipf & Stock, 2013.

Downs, David J. *Alms: Charity, Reward, and Atonement in Early Christianity*. Waco, TX: Baylor University Press, 2016.

Finn, Richard. *Almsgiving in the Later Roman Empire: Christian Promise and Practice 313–450*. Oxford: Oxford University Press, 2006.

Holman, Susan R. *The Hungry Are Dying: Beggars and Bishops in Roman Cappadocia*. Oxford Studies in Historical Theology. Oxford: Oxford University Press, 2001.

_____, ed. *Wealth and Poverty in Early Church and Society*. Grand Rapids: Baker Academic, 2008.

Leemans, Johan, Brian J. Matz, and Johan Verstraeten, eds. *Reading Patristic Texts on Social Ethics: Issues and Challenges for Twenty-First-Century Christian Social Thought*. Washington, DC: Catholic University of America Press, 2011.

Rhee, Helen. *Loving the Poor, Saving the Rich: Wealth, Poverty, and Early Christian Formation*. Grand Rapids: Baker Academic, 2012.

Index

abundance, xxxi, 2, 5, 19, 34, 41, 56, 61, 74, 82, 83, 90, 94, 142, 152

affluence/affluent, xxi, 15, 17, 106

almsgiving/alms/alms deeds, xiv, xv, xvi, xix, xxii–xxiii, xxv, xxvii–xxviii, xxxii, xxxiii, xxxv–xxxvi, xxxviii, xxxix, xliii, xliv–xlv, 41, 42, 43–46, 52n2, 56, 68, 69, 89, 93–94, 96, 99, 107–8, 123n8, 135, 136–37, 143–44, 145, 149, 153, 154; redemptive almsgiving, xxxvi, xxvii, xxxv; as forgiving, 136; as holy usury, xliv. *See also* charity; generosity; giving/ give; good works

ascetic[s], xxxii–xxxiii, xxxiv, xliii, xl–xli, xlv, 29n4, 120n6, 123n8, 125n10

asceticism, xxv, xxxviii, xlv

avarice, xiii, xv, 67, 88, 92, 112–13, 144, 145, 147. *See also* greed

baptism, xviii, xix–xx, xxiv, xxxix, xli, 28, 29, 43, 44, 126

blessing/blessings, xiii, xvii, 18, 28, 33, 47, 64, 98, 137, 153

captive(s), 51, 53, 72, 111, 126, 142

charity, xn2, xvi, xxvii, xxx, xxxi, xxxii, 37–8, 48, 58, 89, 99, 137, 145, 162; works of charity, xxii, xlii, 34, 43, 143. *See also* almsgiving; generosity; giving; good works

children, xxxiv, 26, 40, 45, 51, 58–9, 62, 64–6, 72, 95, 98, 125–26, 132–33, 135, 150; of the earth, 106; of God, 2, 3, 10, 19, 20, 43, 46, 47, 50; of lawlessness, 1

Christ, xvi, xxiii, xxi, xxiii, xxiv, xxv, xxviin17, xxviii,

See also almsgiving; charity; generosity; good works

God, vii, xvi, xviii, xxii, xxiv, xxv–xxviii, xxix–xxx, xli, 2, 5–6, 7, 8, 11, 12, 14, 16–17, 18, 25, 27, 28, 29, 36, 41, 42, 44–45, 48, 53, 60, 64, 80, 81, 84, 95–96, 102, 110, 116, 120, 124, 138, 139, 141, 150, 152; blessing from, xiii, 47, 56; care for the poor, xiii; commandment of, xxv, 15, 17, 44, 108, 121, 143; as creator, xxv, xxxv, 2, 33, 34, 35, 49, 60, 66, 69, 83, 88, 139; as debtor, xxviii, 48, 68, 109; as defender of the poor, xiv, 74; equality in, 50, 79, 82, 129; faith/hope in, ix, xvii–xviii, xix, xliii, 123, 125, 134; forgiveness of, 42; generosity of, 66, 68, 73, 78, 82, 88, 90, 101, 102, 110, 122, 137, 142; goodness of 56, 83, 147; grace of, xxviii, 27, 124, 154; image of, xxxvi, 52, 98, 110; imitation of, xxxvii, 21, 48, 84; in the poor, 137; as judge, xxvii, xxx, 7, 9, 34, 39, 41, 53, 56, 58, 75, 88, 93, 108, 138; justice (providence) of, xx, xxxiv, 60, 107, 129; kingdom of, xv, xxi, xxvii, 10, 17, 40, 63; love of, xxxvii, 9, 20, 68, 89, 155; loving God, 18–19, 151; as master, 4, 8, 16, 31, 58, 64, 66, 122; mercy of, xx, xxviii, 3, 41–42, 43, 44, 55, 84, 143, 145; ownership of, xxvi, 36, 74, 82, 95, 101; righteousness of, xiv, 12; serving God, xv, xxxvii, 3, 4, 5, 48; word of, 150, 152, 155. *See also* children, of God

goods, xi, xli, xlii, 14, 20, 29, 30, 41, 57, 62, 65, 69, 81, 82, 95, 99, 105, 115, 117, 119, 123–25, 127–28, 130, 133–35, 136, 142, 146; as being given by God, 57, 69; earthly, xxvii, 20–21, 37, 47–48, 69, 77, 92, 133–35, 147; heavenly, 20–21, 25–28, 37, 48, 95, 147; worldly, 14, 37, 77, 99–100. *See also* possessions; riches; wealth; use

good works, xvi, xxii, xxv, 8, 19, 41, 42, 47, 48, 58, 66, 78, 110, 113 122, 124, 144. *See also* almsgiving; charity; generosity; giving

greed, xi, xiii, xvi, xxii, xxvi–xxvii, xl, 56, 59, 64, 71, 74, 79, 83, 88, 100, 105–7, 110, 112, 132, 146. *See also* avarice

Holy Spirit, xviii, xxxv, 43–5
homeless, the, xxxvii, 13, 44, 72, 107
hospitality, xv, xvi, 51, 126, 138, 140
humility, 9, 77, 81, 107, 136, 137

134; giving of, xxvi, xlv, 53,
61; heavenly, xxxii, 84, 133;
of the church, xxx–xxxi,
154; love of, xiii, 61, 99;
renunciation of, xxi, xxii,
12–13, 14, 17, 53; spiritual-
ization of, xxii, 15. *See also*
goods; riches; possessions;
use; poverty, in relation to
wealth
wealthy, the, x, xv, xx, xxvi,
xxviii, xxxi, xxxii, xxxiii,
xxxviii, 9, 17–18, 46, 61, 80,
84, 94–95, 113, 127; apostasy
by, xxvi–xxvii (39–42);
denunciation of, xiv; hope
for, 18; salvation of, 8,
10–21; treatment of, 7–9
wickedness/wicked, the, xiv,
xxxviii, 1, 2, 53, 56, 71–72,
89, 93, 107, 136, 138. *See also*
rich, the, wicked
widow[s], xiii, xiv, xxxvii, xlv,
4, 25, 51, 77, 79, 95, 112,
116n2; widow's mite, 73, 94

Zacchaeus, xv, 13, 78

.